THE COURAGE TO FEEL

The Courage to Feel

BUDDHIST PRACTICES FOR
OPENING TO OTHERS

Rob Preece

SNOW LION PUBLICATIONS
ITHACA, NEW YORK

Snow Lion Publications
P.O. Box 6483
Ithaca, New York 14851 USA
(607) 273-8519
www.snowlionpub.com

Printed in USA on acid-free recycled paper.

ISBN-10: 1-55939-333-5
ISBN-13: 978-1-55939-333-1

Library of Congress Cataloging-in-Publication Data

Preece, Rob.
The courage to feel : Buddhist practices for opening
to others / Rob Preece.
p. cm.
Includes bibliographical references.
ISBN-13: 978-1-55939-333-1 (alk. paper)
ISBN-10: 1-55939-333-5 (alk. paper)
1. Compassion—Religious aspects—Buddhism.
2. Religious life—Buddhism. I. Title.
BQ4360.P74 2009
294.3'5677—dc22
2009020750

Designed and typeset by Gopa & Ted2, Inc.

Contents

Acknowledgments

I WISH TO DEDICATE this book to my foremost spiritual guide, Lama Thubten Yeshe, whose quality of heart was so all-embracing; to Lama Zopa Rinpoche, who is an impeccable example of a life dedicated to the welfare of others; and to Gen Jhampa Wangdu, who demonstrated the supreme selflessness of the gift of his life.

I wish to thank Anna, my wife, for her hours of patience and support in reading through this work to help correct and clarify what I have written. I would like to thank Diana England for tirelessly transcribing many of the recorded talks that form the basis for part of this text. I would also like to offer my appreciation for all those I have worked with in retreat, mentoring, and psychotherapy who have shared their experiences, and helped me value the gift of the human heart.

Introduction

THE STORY IS TOLD that when Avalokiteshvara, the Buddha of compassion, was looking at the lives of human beings upon this planet, he saw how much pain and suffering we inflict upon each other, and for a moment his compassion faltered. He almost abandoned his vow to liberate us from suffering. At that instant, his body exploded into a thousand pieces, represented in the image of the thousand-armed Avalokiteshvara. If this can happen to the figure who, in Buddhism, most exemplifies compassion, then perhaps we can be forgiven for not always finding it easy to sustain a compassionate heart in the face of so much suffering in the world.

We may live in times when material, economic, and scientific progress is moving at a rate never before seen, yet our capacity to live peacefully alongside each other seems to remain elusive. When confronted with the constant evidence of so much brutality and corruption present in the world, whether this is seen on the news or experienced closer to home, it is common to feel a sense of anger and outrage, and to feel powerless to do anything to change the ignorance, greed, and hatred that motivate most of the atrocities our fellow humans inflict upon each other. Are we, individually or collectively, able to go beyond the dominance of our instinctual selfishness that reaps so much harm?

What has been all too apparent in my own relationship to the suffering I see in the world is that compassion and loving-kindness are not easy qualities to develop successfully. When faced with the magnitude of suffering and the depth of our human capacity to harm each other and the planet, it is no surprise that on occasions I can feel despair.

Fortunately, there are people who do have the courage to face the world with compassion, rather than perpetuate ill will and hostility. One of the most inspiring examples of this is H.H. the Dalai Lama, who, having endured much personal hardship, and also having witnessed intimately the harm inflicted upon his Tibetan people, responds not with brutal aggression but with humility and care, even towards those who have perpetrated such destruction. This does not render him powerless or impotent to respond. Rather, he continues to actively promote a sense of compassion and care in the world.

Some people seem to have a natural, spontaneous gift of compassion and loving-kindness, and appear genuinely to be able to consider the welfare of others before themselves. This generosity of heart usually comes from a healthy sense of self and a natural capacity to go beyond self-interest. Then there are others who, like myself, have to work at opening the heart to be more caring and sensitive to our fellow travelers on this path, because it does not come so naturally.

If we are to cope with a turbulent and troubled world, and with challenges in our daily lives that can push us to the limit, the solution has to be an inner one. When I reflect on my own life, I can see that two potential choices are there whenever I am really challenged. I could contract into an increasingly fearful, defensive, self-preoccupied place where I become obsessed by security and a sense of my own self-preservation—the idea that I need to look after number one at any cost. Alternately, I could begin to open and see that I am not alone in this plight and that others are suffering too. I could open my heart to the struggle in others' lives and hold an understanding that we are all equal in wishing to be happy and free of suffering.

If we do not find it easy to have compassion, we may wish to ask ourselves: why not? If we find ourselves constantly pulled back into self-preoccupation, what is it that keeps us in this state? What are the emotional and psychological issues that prevent us from opening our hearts to others? What is it that will also help us to take the step of going beyond egocentricity?

Whatever spiritual tradition we may be part of, if we wish to live our lives with greater openness to others, and with the courage and heart to cope with adverse conditions, we have much to learn from the path of the *bodhisattva*. The bodhisattva, sometimes translated as "the awakening warrior," dedicates his or her life to the welfare of others and is willing to face the challenges of life to do so. The bodhisattva's way of life does not lead to a spiritual escape from the reality of the world. Rather, the bodhisattva cultivates the capacity to live within the raw reality of suffering on the ground and transform life's adverse circumstances into a path of awakening. A bodhisattva makes a clear decision to remain embodied and in relationship to life even while reaching states of awareness that go far beyond our normal reality. Such a person is said to renounce the peace of *nirvana* and overcome the fear of *samsara*. What gives this attitude to life a particular significance is that it recognizes that only through fully awakening our innate wholeness can we achieve the greatest benefit to others.

Central to this approach to life is a quality of intention called *bodhichitta*, often translated as "the awakening mind." The awakening mind is most often described as the clear, compassionate intention to attain the state of buddhahood for the welfare of all sentient beings. While "the awakening mind" may seem like a relatively simple phrase, its actual psychological, emotional, and social implications are huge. It is a reorientation of the whole of an individual's direction and meaning in life, rooted in a deep sense of compassion and responsibility towards the welfare of the world.

Our capacity to benefit others will come from a deepening experience of self-realization within the psychological process of what Jung called "individuation." If we consider individuation[1] to be the maturation and embodiment of our innate potential, then the bodhisattva exemplifies this journey in the context of Buddhist life. Jung described how individuation takes us beyond the ego's place of dominance towards an awakening of a deeper center of wholeness. In this process he saw that individuation awakens a more profound relationship to purpose and meaning in our lives. Jung also recognized that as the process progresses, it brings a natural desire to serve the common good, going beyond ego-centeredness.

In Buddhist terms, this altruistic intention to awaken and individuate is bodhichitta, the essence of awakening. How this quality then manifests in the world will depend upon the personality and abilities of the individual. There is no set prescription for how a bodhisattva should live in the world, but the cultivation and refinement of the desire to benefit others are at the heart of all he or she does. What we can learn from the bodhisattva's example is a way of life that responds to the fears and threats of our time not with aggression and self-preoccupation, but with a genuine sense of concern and service.

While compassion and loving-kindness may be innate potentials within each of us, they are often buried beneath layers of emotional wounding. This wounding may not be obvious and may be hard to resolve. Even so, this wounding needs to be faced. The Buddha saw that the causes of suffering lay in the twin roots of selfishness and ignorance and that with the right guidance, we might all find a state of inner peace and happiness. To paraphrase Shantideva, we all seek happiness but endlessly create the causes of suffering.[2] The Buddha recognized that while there is a clear cause of suffering, there can also be a real cessation of suffering, if only we know how to go about it.

Drawing on a number of traditional Buddhist sources, including Shantideva's *Guide to the Bodhisattva's Way of Life* and Lama Tsong-kha-pa's *Great Treatise on the Stages of the Path to Enlightenment*, I wish to explore the cultivation of the compassionate heart of awakening from a psychological viewpoint. I will try to describe the steps to cultivating this quality, including traditional Buddhist meditations, while looking at their psychological and emotional implications. While these meditation practices are found within the Buddhist tradition, this does not imply they are useful only for Buddhists. The understanding gained from this approach can be instrumental for anyone wishing to genuinely expand their experience of compassion, easing their own suffering in the process.

Much of what I have written here has come from the numerous occasions I received instruction on the cultivation of bodhichitta from lamas such as H.H. the Dalai Lama, Lama Thubten Yeshe, and Lama Zopa Rinpoche. It has also arisen from my own exploration of the meditation practices associated with cultivating bodhichitta. I have drawn on the invaluable resource of the experience of those I have worked with in psychotherapy and taught in retreat to look at the psychological effect of such practices. What has emerged over time is a growing sense of the kind of psychological issues these meditation practices provoke and how those issues may be addressed. This is not to say that psychological or emotional issues are in any way detrimental to the practice; indeed, they are part of the natural process unfolding in generating compassion. One might even consider that if these issues are not brought out, perhaps the practices are not touching us as deeply as they might. Recognizing these emotional and psychological issues, however, enables us to pass through them and become free to experience the growth of loving-kindness and compassion in a deep and genuine way.

I am aware, in common with the views of writers such as Ken Wilber, that meditation is not the solution to all of our emotional problems. There are many aspects of our psychological wounding that are only able to be addressed when they are brought out in relationship. The depth experienced in meditation does not necessarily invoke this material, which is partly why some experienced meditators can still have unresolved psychological issues. The particular meditations I wish to describe in this book can, however, begin to address some of these issues. They are not the "cure all" some of us may wish for in meditation practice, but they offer some extremely valuable ways of looking at personal psychological material.

This book includes, therefore, a sequence of meditations that come from traditional Tibetan sources but which I have modified in small ways to make them more psychologically relevant to us in the West. There is no fixed or definitive way to do these practices, but if we are creative and we can find ways of meditating that truly affect us, we may resolve some of the psychological and emotional issues that often block our experience. As an aspect of "skillful means," what we are trying to do is enable the gradual awakening of the qualities of love, compassion, and bodhichitta that can be seen as a natural expression of who we are. Once these qualities begin to grow, they will become part of the undercurrent of our lives. We can begin to be able to genuinely transform adversity into a path of awakening, just as the bodhisattvas of the past have done.

CHAPTER ONE

The Awakening Warrior

THROUGHOUT HISTORY there have been individuals who have demonstrated an extraordinary willingness and courage to dedicate their lives to the welfare of others. While most of these have not been Buddhists and many of them have not even been particularly religious, they could nevertheless be seen as examples of the bodhisattva, the "awakening warrior." While the traditional notion of the bodhisattva may be understood as one who aspires to become awakened in order to benefit others, if we do not bind our view too tightly to the notion of buddhahood as the goal, then the bodhisattva can be seen in many walks of life and in many spiritual traditions. The quality that seems most exemplary in these people is the desire to dedicate their lives to the service of others.

It is easy to consider that originators of spiritual traditions embodied the bodhisattva ideal. The Christian Jesus of Nazareth and Guru Nanak of the Sikh religion would be, in this respect, obvious examples. We can also look to more recent times and see that there have been significant examples of this way of life, such as Gandhi and Nelson Mandela.

There are, however, many other historical and contemporary examples of persons possessing this quality of intention that have not been so famous or in the public eye. Those who follow the path of the bodhisattva can go relatively unnoticed and indeed, this is probably how most would prefer to be, as they seldom would wish for fame and acclaim for their work. The example I think of is a woman named Bunty Wills who lived in London and worked as a therapist and mentor for many people. My memory of her was of a woman who had found the capacity to give herself totally to the service of others who were in need of psychological help. She would see many people each day and had a schedule that began early in the morning. After a period of meditation, she would have a brief breakfast and then people would begin to come. By the end of the day, I have no idea how many people she may have seen, but they were all coming to her because they needed help of some sort. I knew her personally and once asked how she managed to do what she did without feeling exhausted by it. Her answer was that she had long ago given herself up to serve others, and this gave her a huge amount of energy.

Bunty was, for me, an extraordinary example of someone who would try to care for whoever needed help. She was the unconditional mother who had a depth of love and wisdom that in itself was healing to all who came to see her. She made no claims to be particularly religious, although I was aware that her psychological roots were in Jung and her spiritual link was in part to Buddhism. However, she was of a disposition that did not hold strictly to the need for a clearly defined form of spirituality; her spirituality was in the core of her being.

I see Bunty Wills as an illustration of the bodhisattva ideal because my sense was that the heart of her concern was to help others along the journey, just as a shepherd would guide his flock. There was always a sense of concern that her "children" were okay and not lost in the wilderness of life. Many of those she saw were deeply wounded and in need of a parental presence that was always there to watch over them. This she seemed to be able to do with amazing care and concern, seldom seeming to think of her own welfare.

To illustrate the dedication and courage of the bodhisattva, there is another example I wish to give of a man who was willing to actually give his own life for the welfare of others. In 1981 I was fortunate enough to be introduced to a monk living close to Tushita Retreat Center near McLeod Ganj in Himachal Pradesh, north India. This monk was called Gen Jhampa Wangdu and was to become an extremely important mentor for me in my period of retreats while in

India. Gen Jhampa Wangdu, or Genla as I called him, was in his fifties when we met and had not long before come down the mountain from his retreat hut, where he had been in retreat for many years. From his childhood, Genla was unusual in that he was placed in the monastery at about the age of six or seven, but did not seem to be particularly comfortable there. At Sera Je, his monastery near Lhasa in Tibet, he was often seen as something of a troublemaker. He had fights with the other young monks and did not seem to study well.

When in 1959 he left Tibet with a group of other relatively young monks, he arrived in Buxaduar, northeast India, where conditions were extremely hard. The monks were poor and it was very hot. They had travelled a vast distance and many of them had suffered hugely on the journey. Soon after his arrival in India, however, Genla's frustration with being in a monastic situation grew. He did not like this environment and wanted to leave. Eventually, he did indeed leave and found a place in the mountains nearby where he could go into retreat. He was very dedicated to a lama called Trichang Rinpoche, who guided him in his practice, and soon began to embark on a journey of retreats that would last about twenty-five years.

During this time, he moved to Dharamsala and continued retreat in a hut very close to where I was in retreat, high in the foothills overlooking McLeod Ganj and the Dalai Lama's residence and monastery. When I met him, he had come down the mountain because his health had begun to fail during one of his retreats.

Genla had by this time become well respected amongst his friends as a very highly realized yogi who had tremendous devotion to the Dalai Lama. Over the next period of years, I was fortunate to study some important tantric practices with him, something that was rare because he did not accept disciples. My root teacher, Lama Thubten Yeshe, who was a close friend of Genla's, eventually persuaded him to teach me.

It was while I was in a period of retreat that Genla also entered a particular retreat for a period of around nine months. I learned from Lama Zopa Rinpoche only later that he had gone into retreat to do a practice that was intended to take on a particular karmic hindrance to the Dalai Lama's life. This was, obviously, kept very quiet.

Later, when Genla had finished his retreat I learned that whatever he had been doing was successful, but I had no idea of the implications. Within a relatively short space of time, Genla caught pneumonia and died of a stroke. I was fortunate in being able to sit with his body during the next three days, while it was clear from the feeling present in his room that he was still in meditation, even though clinically dead. After three days the room suddenly changed, and Lama Zopa Rinpoche said that Genla's consciousness had gone.

I was profoundly affected by this experience and felt that someone extremely important to me had gone, at least physically. The quality of love and care that I felt with Genla was something I had seldom felt in anyone that close to my life. He was very ordinary and humble in his life and yet made a profound offering of his life so that the person he considered to be of so great an importance to the world could live. Such is the life of one unknown bodhisattva.

We may not be able to live with exactly the same sense of selflessness that seems so present in the examples I have given. As models of a way of life that we might aspire to, they are nevertheless very valuable. Each of us in our own way can begin to cultivate some of the qualities of the bodhisattva. We can do so in our own particular way that makes the greatest use of our own particular qualities. This does not have to be in grand statements or through public acclaim. This is not the point.

It is important to remember that the bodhisattva is not an iconic ideal of perfection. It is more the model of what, within our humanity, could be seen as a noble and wholesome way of life. Throughout history, the bodhisattva is one who has found within the capacity to embody love, compassion, and the willingness to dedicate life to the welfare of others. Perfection does not play a part in this aspiration, other than perhaps on the Buddhist path with the ideal of buddhahood as a goal.

The bodhisattva is not yet a buddha and still remains within the realm of human limitation. In the lives of bodhisattvas, therefore, it is probably best not to expect to see miracles and spectacular demonstrations of spiritual prowess. There can be something remarkably ordinary in the life of someone who is embodying a grounded spirituality in the world and devotion to serving others. Yet within that ordinariness is a capacity to live in troubled times and respond not with defensiveness and fear but with genuine compassion, consideration, and care for the welfare of others. In Buddhist language this quality is called *bodhichitta*.

CHAPTER TWO

Bodhichitta

WHEN I FIRST encountered the two Tibetan lamas who became my teachers, in 1973, I was at a meditation course at Kopan near Kathmandu in Nepal. I was immediately in awe of the complexity and profundity of the teachings I was receiving. They seemed to provide answers to questions that had been disturbing me for years. But this was not what had the deepest impact upon me. What really touched me was a feeling these lamas *gave off,* which I had never encountered before. It was a powerful, almost palpable feeling of kindness and care with a sense of generosity that seemed to be totally dedicated to the welfare of those I was with. I found myself completely beguiled by their quality of heart and hungry for its warmth. It was only in the course of time that I began to understand that this quality actually had a name—bodhichitta, sometimes called "the awakening mind." I discovered that bodhichitta was central to these lamas' attitude towards others, and I began to learn that, as a quality of heart, it can sustain our own capacity to cope with life's troubles as well as benefit others. One of these lamas was teaching that just a momentary thought of bodhichitta pacifies the mind and heals confusion. It is like the dawning moon of the mind that dispels the darkness of our suffering.[3]

Bodhichitta is like the motor that powers the bodhisattva's life, and from a Buddhist point of view, without it there is no potential to become a buddha. We could say that without the Buddha there would be no *dharma,* and without the dharma it is extremely difficult to overcome suffering. For this reason, according to all the major authorities on Mahayana Buddhism such as Nagarjuna, Asanga, and Atisha, bodhichitta is more important than any other aspect of the entire Buddhist path. In his *Guide to the Bodhisattva's Way of Life,* Shantideva says that bodhichitta is "the quintessential butter from the churning of the milk of the Dharma."[4]

While we may each have the potential for bodhichitta within us, its full awakening is not something that arises easily or, according to Shantideva, that often. He says:

> Just like a flash of lightening on a dark cloudy night
> For an instant brightly illuminates all,
> Likewise in this world, through the might of Buddha,
> A wholesome thought rarely and briefly appears.[5]

Whereas the dark, cloudy night of ignorance that keeps us within the cycle of existence can continue eternally, the intention to benefit all sentient beings may arise only for a moment and yet has far-reaching consequences. It is a spark of illumination and hope that offers the possibility of total liberation from suffering.

It is said that many eons earlier, at the time of the Buddha Kashyapa, the spark of bodhichitta arose in the mind of a being in hell who was to become a bodhisattva and the future Shakyamuni Buddha. This hell-being saw another pulling a huge load with ropes and suddenly felt great compassion for his suffering. He took the ropes with the intention of pulling the load himself but, according to one explanation of this story, was beaten to death by hell-guardians and was reborn in a fortunate rebirth. From that time, his compassionate intention developed like an acorn growing into a mighty oak tree. This being eventually became the Buddha Shakyamuni and gave us the gift of the dharma.

The term *bodhichitta* comprises two syllables: *bodhi* meaning awakening and *chitta* meaning mind, heart, or essence. In principle, one could therefore translate bodhichitta as "the awakening mind," or the "essence of awakening." The reason we say that *chitta* represents the heart and mind together is because, whereas in the West we think of the mind as up in the head, from a Tibetan Buddhist point of view, the root of the mind is in the heart, or more specifically, the heart *chakra*. To say that the heart or mind is waking up, however, does not convey a sense of what the quality of bodhichitta is. Neither does saying that it is the intention to attain buddhahood for the benefit of sentient beings. This can sound somewhat simplistic and in no way conveys the depth of meaning and strength of feeling that lies within bodhichitta. Even the most frequent translation, "the awakening mind," does not convey the real sense of bodhichitta and for this reason, throughout this book, I have chosen to stay with the term *bodhichitta*.

When I first began to receive teachings on bodhichitta from different lamas, I found I was somewhat mystified by what seemed to be more than just a kind of intellectual motivation. It felt like yet another kind of trying and striving that engaged the same tendency as striving to do more lengths of the pool or striving for perfection. Bodhichitta in this respect could be just another intellectual idea or ego intention that did not come from a particularly profound inner place. I felt I was missing the point.

I was in Bodhgaya in December 1980 with a group of Westerners receiving teachings on Shantideva's *Guide to the Bodhisattva's Way of Life* from a lama called Tara Tulku. One day I went to him privately and asked, "If bodhichitta is the thought to get enlightened for the benefit of all sentient beings—this kind of intention—what would it *feel* like?" He looked at me intently with wide open eyes and suddenly I felt an incredible rush of energy. It was extraordinary—like being burst open with an immensely powerful flood of feeling in the heart. Feelings of love and joy and a sensation of bliss rushed through me. After a couple of minutes he switched it off again and sat back with a radiant grin on his golden face. I realized that this was not some intellectual idea; it was a felt opening of something that totally reshapes one's experience and one's view of the world. I left the room and thought: that was a good answer to my question. Thank you very much. Where do I get more of this? How do I cultivate this quality?

At that time I was aware of my limited capacity for being in touch with feelings that were not clouded by strong emotions,[6] and my notions of the heart were still somewhat immature. I could understand the reasoning behind the idea of bodhichitta but was only beginning to see that it held something that brought together heart and reason as well as vision and a pragmatic realism.[7]

Although we may think of *cultivating* bodhichitta, it is important to remember that it is an innate potential within us. It is not something we lack and therefore have got to find or receive from outside. As the "awakening mind," it is the awakening of an innate quality in each of us. I have sometimes heard friends say they feel they could never really develop bodhichitta because it is beyond them. This way of thinking about ourselves is very limiting when we all have the capacity to feel care and concern for another's welfare. Therefore, the question may be: what is it that is preventing this capacity from growing, and how do we actually cultivate it? Because it *is* something latent within, when I asked Tara Tulku my question about the felt experience of bodhichitta, he facilitated a momentary taste.

Bodhichitta is one of those mysteries that is not easy to describe. Because it is hard to describe the true meaning of this quality, Shanitdeva uses many poetic metaphors:

> It is the supreme ambrosia
> That overcomes the sovereignty of death,
> It is the inexhaustible treasure
> That eliminates all poverty in the world.
> It is the supreme medicine
> That quells the world's disease.
> It is the tree that shelters all beings
> Wandering and tired on the path of conditioned existence.
> It is the universal bridge
> That leads to freedom from unhappy states of birth,
> It is the dawning moon of the mind
> That dispels the torment of disturbing conceptions.
> It is the great sun that finally removes
> The misty ignorance of the world...[8]

Bodhichitta can be seen as a blend of flavors that make up the whole meal. The different aspects of bodhichitta that I describe in what follows can also be viewed as the different facets of a precious jewel. Each facet in itself is not bodhichitta, but when brought together as a *gestalt,* they create a whole that is far greater than the individual facets alone. It is in part a quality of intention that is extremely potent and that is not ego-based. It is a kind of heartfelt yearning. It is a deeply felt quality of opening to something that is like a "calling" or dedication. There is a sense of vocation that says this is *it,* what else is there to do?

Bodhichitta as Universal Compassion and Love

Bodhichitta grows from the roots of compassion, and compassion comes from recognition of our human frailty and the struggle we have in life; it does not come from ideals of perfection.[9] The bodhisattva has compassion towards our fallibility and understands that we are all seeking to be happy and yet endlessly create the causes for suffering. We cannot experience compassion unless we have suffered ourselves, because it requires a level of empathy that arises because we also know what it is like to feel a certain way or experience a certain kind of problem. Compassion can also motivate us to do more than simply feel compassionate. The compassion contained within bodhichitta is not just the wish that others be free of suffering; it is an active intention to engage in the release of others from suffering.

There are times when our sensitivity to the suffering around us can lead to a feeling of compassion that is hard to bear. It can also lead to the feeling that there is nothing we can do to help. What our experience of compassion needs at these times is a natural channel for its unfolding to mitigate against our feelings of powerlessness and impotence. Bodhichitta gives a sense of possibility. It is the channel through which our compassion has a natural potential to be expressed and realized. In the expression of bodhichitta, compassion becomes a vast, unconditional, universal, and all-embracing quality like the "supreme medicine" or the "tree that shelters all." Although compassion does not specifically have buddhahood as its intention, once it is conjoined with the vision of wholeness represented in buddhahood, bodhichitta emerges.

As our experience of compassion grows, we can see that it has two components: one specifically focused upon someone's suffering, the other vast and spacious, without a specific reference. The focused aspect of compassion between one person and another, or relative compassion, is held within a greater sense of what could be called universal compassion. This universal compassion is something we can feel as a quality of presence that is unconditional and vast. It is like the moisture in the atmosphere that can pervade our experience of life and then focus into a droplet that is immediate and personal. It is that capacity to remain open and yet be ready to respond at any moment to whatever or whoever is there.

I have felt these two aspects of compassion in relation to the Dalai Lama. In a large group of people, he holds the space with a quality of compassion that is almost tangible and yet not specific to anyone. If someone should come up to him, the attention of care and concern for that person is total. What sometimes astonishes me about the Dalai Lama is the ease with which he can shift from one position to the other.

We can see the same dual nature with loving-kindness. It can be like the warmth of sunlight that pervades the atmosphere and shines upon us equally without discrimination. It can also be like a beam of light that focuses its gaze upon an individual and creates a sense of personal love and care.

Both of these qualities were very apparent to me with my teacher Lama Thubten Yeshe. His quality of love was something that radiated from him as a presence of what he would sometimes call a "big heart." To sit in his presence on occasions when he was teaching was to be held in a sense of warmth and love that was not focused upon anyone in particular. It pervaded the environment with a quality that nourished the soul. In his presence I would sometimes feel that his love seemed to make life feel easier, like a kind of nectar that would soften the pain.

When I visited him privately this quality would feel immediately focused upon me. I would feel the focus of his attention as if I were, at that moment, the most important person in the world. I would go with all manner of questions that I wanted him to sort out for me. In his presence they seemed to melt away, as though I was given a deep sense that all was fine. It was a profound quality of acceptance and care "like a loving parent for his only child."[10]

Lama Yeshe's quality of heart was so great, his willingness to embrace all those he came in contact with so unconditional, that he deeply affected those who met him. There was a certain irony in that his physical heart was so vulnerable. He suffered a heart condition that would cause his heart to swell up and fill his chest cavity, making breathing very difficult. It was as though his spiritual heart was so vast that his physical heart could barely sustain him. Even so, he would give himself totally to caring for others with a huge heart.

While we are contracted into our own suffering and needs, we can barely respond to others. With bodhichitta the capacity of the heart to love opens and grows. We begin to express a natural warmth, a genuine heartfelt concern and care for others. In time this can express the universal, unconditional quality of love and compassion that is present within bodhichitta.

Bodhichitta as a Greater Perspective

There are times in our daily lives when we become trapped in a limited, narrow perspective that turns our experiences into a torment. We become so obsessively bound up in the small view of our life that we are unable to let go. Things become painful and fraught with distress because we are unable to raise our awareness from the hole we have dug ourselves into. When we have this disposition we can become negative and cynical because all we can see are the faults and flaws in our life.

There is an expansion of awareness in bodhichitta as the mind opens. The "openness mind"[11] doesn't get caught up in small-minded, narrow, limited views. It is a *big* mind that doesn't contract into the pettiness that is so obsessed with "my problems" that we fail to see a bigger picture. Our personal life problems can seem insignificant when placed alongside the suffering of so many.

When we open our attention to the bigger picture and see the broader context of our own and others' lives, it begins to put our experience into perspective. As a psychotherapist I became acutely aware of this when the tsunami in Southeast Asia killed hundreds of thousands of people at Christmas 2004 and when the hurricane devastated New Orleans in 2005. These events highlighted the disparity between times when we are caught in a painful, narrow sense of our lives, and the enormity of collective suffering. I can personally feel a great sense of liberation when I place my own troubles in the context of the bigger picture; they seem relatively small and insignificant.

The expansion of awareness that is an aspect of bodhichitta can open us to a view of reality and the suffering of others that puts our own suffering into perspective. It counters the disposition to contract into a small-minded, obsessive view of ourselves in our life.

Bodhichitta and a Vision of Wholeness

The quality of intention that comes with the experience of bodhichitta is focused around what we might describe as a vision of wholeness. We may see this vision in two ways. One is in the recognition that the goal of the bodhisattva's path is buddhahood, the state of total awakening. On another level, the vision of wholeness arises from the knowledge that our innate potential is the primordially pure quality of our buddha nature. The former of these relies upon some level of understanding what buddhahood implies as a goal. The second, however, can be experienced more directly as an inner knowing, a kind of intuitive sense of what our innate potential is; or as a symbolic vision of wholeness.

Even though we may have studied the teachings that describe a buddha's qualities, we can still only imagine what it might be like to be a buddha. The impact a symbolic vision of wholeness has upon us, however, can be immediate and profound. It can bypass the intellectual disposition that wants knowledge.

I recall the effect a statue of the Buddha had upon me when I was in my early teens. At that time I had no relationship to Buddhism and yet seeing a figure seated in a state of such sublime serenity deeply affected me. The same resonance occurred when in my early twenties I spent many hours drawing and painting symmetrical patterns of flowers and seed heads. These mandalalike forms had a deep influence upon me even though I had little or no understanding of what they implied. It was only later as I began to study the work of C. G. Jung on mandalas that I saw why they had such a strong effect upon me.

Jung recognized the profound impact of a vision or symbol of wholeness on the intuitive understanding of our innate nature. He saw that in the journey of individuation, the psyche responds to images that symbolize the archetype of wholeness. He also saw that the unconscious will reveal to us in dreams and active imagination a source of meaning and wholeness in the images of the Self.

Because I will refer to Jung's concept of a Self—as opposed to a self or ego—from time to time, I think it is worth making clear, for those who would consider ideas of a Self contradictory to Buddhist thinking, that Jung did not see the Self as some kind of inherent or self-existent Self. It is a metaphorical center of wholeness that nevertheless has great impact upon our process of individuation. In this sense, the label "Self" may be given to the essential buddha nature we each possess.

Whether we experience outer symbols or inner visions of our potential, they have a profound effect on the psychological roots of our sense of self. A vision of wholeness can bring with it a sense of awe and awaken a depth of inspiration that can feel highly charged and potent. It can bring an inner knowing that is beyond words, as well as a yearning for wholeness. It can also give the sense that we know what we must do. We know what our life purpose is about.

A vision of wholeness is imbued with an energy Jung called "numinous,"[12] a charged awesome attraction to the significance and meaning of the vision. The vitality that comes with these images of totality brings inspiration and motivation. It awakens in us an awareness of a resource that we perhaps had no idea we possessed. For the bodhisattva, bodhichitta derives much of its sense of direction from the inspiration and vitality of such a vision. The vision that lives in the heart of bodhichitta is of our intrinsic buddha nature. This may be expressed as an image of the Buddha seated beneath the bodhi tree at the time of his awakening, or of the various tantric deities and mandalas within the Tibetan tradition. Whatever its form, the vision brings great power and inspiration.

Gaining an intellectual understanding of the qualities of the vision is somewhat irrelevant. It is not intellectual understanding of buddhahood that necessarily brings the inspiration of the vision. Intellectual understanding may help, but it is an inner knowing that comes from this experience that is most powerful. What makes a vision of wholeness meaningful as a source of inspiration is allowing a connection to be made when we let it touch us.

In the *Uttaratantra* by Maitreya, it is said that our recognizing our buddha potential is like a man living in poverty discovering that buried beneath his home is a priceless treasure.[13] It is like discovering a jewel buried in the mud. If our buddha potential is like a golden statue wrapped in filthy rags, the golden image can never be tarnished by the rags—it is merely obscured by them. When I was younger and my understanding of Buddhism was relatively poor, the images that came from this text had a profound effect on me. They gave me an intuitive sense of my intrinsic value in a way that I had never felt previously. The influence of religion in my early years had left me with the belief that I was essentially a sinner and that at the root of my being was an innate badness that I had to overcome. It left me fundamentally unable to trust myself because to let go would be to open up my innate badness. When I met my Tibetan teachers and they spoke of my buddha nature, I felt a huge sense of relief. Perhaps I was not so bad after all, and perhaps when I allowed myself to relax a little and open up, I would find my true nature as something whole and wonderful rather than something to be feared and suppressed.

Our visions of wholeness connect us to what is healthy and positive in our nature. They act as a natural magnet that draws us towards an unfolding of our potential wholeness. It is important to recognize, however, that the notion of wholeness Jung implied in the journey of individuation is subtly different from that of the

Buddhist. For Jung, wholeness was not a state of perfection; it was a state of integration that brought together the different aspects of our nature. The act of integration includes an acknowledgment of our fallibility and our shadow. To be human, he believed, was to have a shadow, and to hold the view that we are otherwise is either seriously inflated or suggests that we have gone beyond our human fallibility.

This may on the surface seem to contradict the notion of wholeness for the Buddhist, in which the Buddha represents a state of perfected awakening and transformation. In effect, a buddha has gone beyond human fallibility in terms of the realization and transformation he or she has attained. A buddha is said to be one who has gone beyond, a *tathagata*, and as such, is no longer bound by the ties of karma and the cycle of existence of which our humanity is so much a part.

For the Buddhist, therefore, one could say there are two possible notions of wholeness: one which might be seen as a process still unfolding, the other a state of ultimate perfection. The first of these is represented by the bodhisattva, who attains a quality of wholeness and integration yet is still subject to human fallibility. A bodhisattva still has a shadow. This idea is like Jung's notion of wholeness. The second is the state of total transformation where a buddha has purified all obscuring defilements and attained a vast wisdom that perceives the nature of reality. The bodhisattva could still be seen as within human relativity, whereas a buddha has gone beyond such limitation. In the etymology of *sang gye*, the Tibetan word for "buddha," *sang* means cleansed or purified and *gye* means to have cultivated vast knowledge.

Bodhichitta as the Heart of Meaning

Sometimes our life can feel devoid of meaning even though we may try in different ways to put meaning into it. We may think that if we do a particular job, become a teacher, a therapist, or a social worker, or have children it will give us meaning. We may hope that if we engage in a particular project it will provide a sense of fulfillment and purpose. In one respect, all of these choices are perfectly valid. They give our conventional life a relatively meaningful sense of direction. Bodhichitta, however, brings an undercurrent of meaning which flows through our life on a deeper level. It gives a quality of meaningful intention that then colors everything else we might do. Perhaps this could be seen as a shift from having a sense of doing something meaningful to living with a sense of meaning.

Jung spoke of the Self as the archetype of wholeness and also of meaning in our life. He saw the Self as the metaphorical center of our totality that deeply informed who we are, whether we are conscious of it or not. He also recognized that those times when we feel alienated from the root of meaning in our life are when we have fallen out of relationship to the Self. We can then feel lost, and life lacks a sense of value, purpose, and direction. This lack of relationship to our life's purpose can lead to physical as well as psychological illness. Jung saw that at certain times in our life the crisis that unfolds is both the result of this alienation and also the process that brings about a restoration of relationship to a deeper source of meaning. When we listen to the Self, however, and allow it to guide us, we will respond to the source of what gives meaning. The "archetypal intent"[14] of the Self will lead us to what is meaningful as we awaken. For this to happen, we must learn to respond to our heart and, as Joseph Campbell put it, to "follow our bliss."

Meaning comes when we go deeply within, wait, listen, and open. It begins to come when we genuinely open to the suffering of those around us with a compassionate heart. Equally, it comes as we respond to the environment within which we live with care and concern. The meaning or purpose to be found in bodhichitta is then less associated with what we do than with the quality we bring to what we engage in. Small, simple aspects of our life can be profoundly meaningful and have deep impact both for ourselves and others. Meaning lies in the quality of heart that we put into what we do.

It is not, therefore, the outer manifestation of what we can achieve that is the root of meaning. It is the undercurrent of bodhichitta's intention or purpose and meaning that flows within. What bodhichitta implies is that in attuning to our buddha nature or buddha potential, we touch a source of meaning in ourselves that will come through whatever we do.

This root of meaning gives the bodhisattva the capacity to live a relatively ordinary life and transform adverse circumstances into the path. Even small things become meaningful, like the way we respond to someone's distress or a gesture of friendliness that lifts someone's day. This deeper sense of purpose is reflected in the care we give to our relationships and the environment. Being present and responsive to what arises may mean that the eventual goal of our sense of purpose is less crucial. We are seldom, if ever, able to see fully where our path will take us, and once we are open to the meaning present in bodhichitta, the ego must surrender ambitions and allow the journey to unfold.

Bodhichitta as a Quality of Courage

Bodhichitta as a quality of the heart can have a further implication in our lives, reflected in the term *bodhisattva*, which can be translated as "the awakening warrior." In the Tibetan phrase *chang chub sem ba*, the term *chang chub* (Sanskrit *bodhi*) means "awakened," *sem* refers to the heart/mind and *ba* implies "warrior." The bodhisattva lives with a quality of heart that engages with life fully, wholeheartedly, and courageously. We can see in the word "courage" the same quality of heart or, in French, *coeur*.

Many times I have heard Lama Zopa Rinpoche say how, through a depth of compassion that finds the suffering of sentient beings unbearable even for one moment, a bodhisattva will descend into the deepest hell even for the sake of one being. Whenever I have heard him say this I have usually felt somewhat inadequate, feeling I was unlikely to be able to cope with such an ordeal. While this left me rather disheartened, feeling my weaknesses were all too apparent, something has changed over the years. I do not think I am ready to enter the deepest hell for one being, but what I have learned is to not judge myself for it and to have a sense of compassion for my own and others' fallibility.

When we look at our lives there are countless ways in which we can easily be caught in a disheartened or fearful place. Shantideva speaks of the bodhisattva as one who heroically faces the inner enemy of the emotional afflictions and will not be defeated by them.[15] Perhaps fear is one of our greatest enemies. The point is not that we should have no fear, but that we should not allow our lives to be dominated by its limiting effects.

In my own life and the lives of many I have worked with in therapy, it has been clear that fear is one of the greatest barriers to engaging with life. It can block us from truly manifesting what we are capable of and cripple our sense of self. We can be given opportunities to fulfill some task that could be extremely beneficial, yet draw back and run away from the challenge. We may fear being seen, being successful, being powerful, or being ourselves. We may half-heartedly take up some project or task and then wonder why it is only partially fulfilling. When this happens it becomes all too easy to give up and abandon what we are working towards, because we do not have the courage to follow it through. As Shantideva says, when we get the habit of not completing what we begin, it weakens our capacity to fulfill our potential.[16]

There is an important quality of the heart that softens and responds with warmth and love. Soft-hearted sentimentality, however, weakens our capacity to benefit others. "Compassion is not sentimentality," Lama Yeshe once said. There is equally the need for the strength and courage of heart to live with passion and clarity of purpose. If we are to take on the bodhisattva's sense of responsibility towards the welfare of others, we need that courage.

With bodhichitta we take heart and our capacity for courage grows. This means we develop the bravery to engage with life and not run away from its challenges. When we put our heart into something, we are fully engaged and committed to what we do. To take on the challenge of the bodhisattva to awaken for the welfare of others, we must have courage to face a journey that will never be easy. As the awakening warrior, the bodhisattva wholeheartedly faces adverse circumstances and transforms them into the path. This can also be seen as a kind of passion for what he or she is living. Living passionately does not mean that life is full of emotional drama, but rather that there is a fire in what we do that comes from the heart and ignites and inspires the sense of engagement.

Bodhichitta can draw together all these qualities of the heart and express them in the capacity to overcome the ego's limiting fears and restrictions. When we can allow ourselves to respond to life with heart, the possibilities of what we can manifest for the welfare of others may be extraordinary.

Bodhichitta as a Source of Transformation

Shantideva describes bodhichitta as being like a gold-making elixir as it transforms our normal limited, relatively defiled state into the state of a buddha.[17] Once bodhichitta is generated it is as though we have within a force for transformation that is going to change us irrevocably and bring inconceivable benefits to others. It is like igniting a fire within that will gradually burn away impurities to reveal the pure substance of our enlightened nature. It is one of the primary ingredients that purifies our own causes for suffering.

In order for us to achieve buddhahood, it is crucial to generate a kind of inner vitality as the power to enable us to accomplish the qualities of transformation. We need to accumulate what is tradi-tionally called "merit," which is simply the generation of our own internal vitality to take us on this journey. Without it, we won't have the energy in the mind or passion in the heart for the demands of the path and for realizations to arise.

The most potent way to generate this vitality is said to be through bodhichitta because this is the quality of intention that turns our worldly actions into virtue. It is this virtuous karma that then generates a potential vitality to transform ourselves and our lives. Once we germinate the seed of bodhichitta, our vitality expands and grows, making us more capable of greater karmic potential. As we practice, it enables us to release more of the vitality that helps bodhichitta to grow still further. Following Shantideva's metaphor of the alchemical process, through practice, in the "heat" of the process, bodhichitta can grow into something very powerful. As a catalyst this quality activates a process of transformation that can bring out our natural creative potential to engage in our life with energy and vision in ways we perhaps could never imagine.

Shantideva also says that the virtue accumulated through the practice of bodhichitta is like no other. It is like a tree that "[u]nceasingly bears fruit and thereby flourishes without end."[18] This means that the power of our actions and the vitality bound up in them will create positive results infinitely. Through bodhichitta we can have the power to transform ourselves and our life.

Bodhichitta as "The Treasure Hard to Attain"

As we have seen, bodhichitta is considered to be perhaps the most crucial ingredient of the Buddhist path. It is interesting that many of the metaphors which repeatedly arise in the teachings of bodhichitta portray it as a kind of treasure with magical properties. Shantideva says:

Just like a blindman
Discovering a jewel in a heap of rubbish,
Likewise, by some coincidence,
An Awakening Mind has been born within me.
It is the supreme ambrosia that overcomes the sovereignty
of death,
It is the inexhaustible treasure that eliminates all poverty
in the world,
It is the supreme medicine that quells the world's disease,
It is the tree that shelters all beings wandering and tired
on the path of conditioned existence.
It is the universal bridge that leads to freedom from unhappy
states of birth,
It is the dawning moon of mind that dispels the torment
of disturbing conceptions,
It is the great sun, which finally removes the misty ignorance
of the world.[19]

When I first read these metaphors I was immediately reminded of what Jung called "the treasure hard to attain."[20] In the language of myth, we may discover "the well at the world's end," the sacred pearl, the elixir of life, the philosopher's stone, the sacred spring, the *fons mecurialis*,[21] and so forth. In the mythical journey these are symbolic objects that often represent the source of transformation or healing. They are sought as a means of healing a malaise or bringing special powers to the hero of the story. There is something about the metaphors used by Shantideva to describe the quality of bodhichitta that has many echoes of this magical "treasure hard to attain." The sense is that once awakened, bodhichitta opens up an experience that has far-reaching, even mystical, implications.

It is particularly within the tantric tradition that we might look to gain a deeper understanding of this aspect of bodhichitta. From a tantric perspective, the "treasure hard to find" may be conceived of as the innate energetic potential within each of us that is released as we awaken. In tantric language, the elemental essences found within the body, known sometimes as drops or in Tibetan *tig le*, are also known as red and white bodhichitta because as they awaken, they give rise to our enlightenment. These drops are usually located at specific places within the body called *chakras*. This energy is particularly connected to the heart chakra such that as the heart chakra opens, the natural energy bound up in the heart is released. Thus, the drops, like the treasure, are aspects of our innate vitality that are at the heart of our potential for transformation.

Our experience of bodhichitta enables us to access a quality in ourselves that brings the power of healing and transformation. From a tantric perspective it is believed that so long as this resource of vitality is not awakened, our physical and emotional health will be subject to constant vulnerability and sickness. Our life can then feel as if it lacks some essential vitality and positive inspiration. This can lead us to feel that we do not have the inner resources to cope with the struggles and stresses of life. Our vulnerability to the presence of negative, destructive, and unhealthy energy in the environment will then make us susceptible to both physical and psychological disease.

From a tantric viewpoint, reconnecting to the source of our innate healing vitality enables us to deal with the turmoil of life from a more balanced and robust place in ourselves. It is said that the bodhisattva is like the peacock that can transform poisonous plants into its brilliant colors. This is a quality that is not easily understood intellectually. It is, however, part of the mystery of bodhichitta that is "the supreme medicine that quells the world's disease."

Bodhichitta as a Surrender of Ego

Bodhichitta as a quality of intention requires us to utterly surrender our normal ego will to a greater purpose. This has sometimes been described as a kind of shift from "I will" to "Thy will be done." While in the Buddhist view there is no external "Thy," nevertheless we could see the shift of intention that comes through surrender as having a similar effect. Jung spoke of the process of individuation as one in which gradually there is a shift of center and the ego lets go to the power and influence of the Self. This surrender to the Self as the root of meaning and wholeness is something that he felt would happen organically, naturally as a part of the individuation process. Indeed, he saw the Self as ultimately demanding that this should happen and creating conditions in our life to enable it. We may think we have a Self, but actually, the Self has us. The most dramatic experience of this kind of event and passage of transformation is when we have a kind of breakdown, or those occasions when the ego must let go and die to enable us to open to the call of the Self. This process will often restore a sense of meaning, purpose, health, and wholeness following a time when the ego had become too rigid, dominant, and unhealthy.

If we translate Jung's understanding into the context of bodhichitta, this means that we come to that moment in our personal journey when we recognize that to dedicate our life to the welfare of others requires a deep letting go. We give ourselves to a sense of meaning that will then unfold in our life in a way over which we may feel we have little control. We must learn to trust in an unfolding process towards our enlightened goal. As we do so, it is like stepping into the river of our life and truly allowing it to carry us. Bodhichitta intention, as an expression of archetypal intent, is that river. It flows beneath our life as a powerful current taking us in a direction we may only partly grasp. As Shantideva writes,

> And for those who have perfectly seized this mind,
> With the thought never to turn away
> From totally liberating
> The infinite forms of life,
> From that time hence,
> Even while asleep or unconcerned,
> A force of merit equal to the sky
> Will perpetually ensue.[22]

Bodhichitta once awakened has the kind of potential behind it such that even if we are asleep or unconscious, we are part of that unfolding process. So whatever we do if we have bodhichitta, it becomes part of our life practice; we don't have to be sitting down meditating all the time or doing formal practices.

In the *Heruka Sadhana* of Pabongka Rinpoche it is written that "in order to eliminate the sufferings of sentient beings I offer myself immediately to all the Buddhas." If we can begin to live our lives in this way, we surrender the ego's will to the intention of all the Buddhas and ask them to manifest whatever is necessary to enable our life to be of benefit to others.

Once bodhichitta is born, whatever we choose to engage in our life can be seen as a manifestation of our buddha potential. We do not have to do something grand or special to be actualizing our buddha nature through the awakening mind. Whether it is the washing up or being a bricklayer, our actions are as valid an expression of our awakening mind as being a great teacher or yogi.

Bodhichitta as a Dynamic Responsibility

Outside the Buddhist world it is often considered that Buddhism is a somewhat passive religion; that Buddhists are introverted and do not actively engage in the world. This perception is in part a reflection of the view that meditation is a more introverted tendency but also arises because of the emphasis in Buddhism on nonattachment. A common image of Buddhism that originally came to the West is of the shaven-headed, saffron-robed monk, detached from the world, living in the forest a life of peaceful serenity free of ego and not concerned by the troubles of this life. We may think of the Buddhist monk who wanders the land with his begging bowl taking only what is given, renouncing any engagement with worldly life. This view has led to the notion that Buddhists do not act with self-determination and will passively accept what happens without reaction.

While there are clear reasons why this view should have grown, and there are some Buddhists who may practice in this way, it is not an accurate picture of Buddhism in general. When I first encountered Tibetan Buddhist monks in Nepal and India, one of the things that felt immediately apparent was their dynamism and vitality. Far from being passive they seemed lively, active, engaged, robust, and very busy, perhaps sometimes too busy.

This could be seen as a reflection of the Tibetans themselves and indeed, this is partly true. As mountain people, their lives have been tough and demanding. They have lived in circumstances that require a level of natural ruggedness and energy to cope with the environment. It could be in part the nature of the style of practice they follow, which is full of ritual and creativity. This is not the only reason for their energetic and active approach to Buddhist life. At the heart of their practice is a dynamic quality of intention that is constantly active in working for the welfare of others. Bodhichitta in this respect creates a creative intention that in many ways suits Western life.

We are very active in the West. Indeed, many of us suffer from what might be seen as a condition of being overactive, where we find it hard to stop. While bodhichitta is not an overactive pathology that can't stop, it nevertheless brings a quality of intention that actively engages in the world to benefit others. This dynamism, contrary to the misconception of Buddhism as a passive religion, will not allow one to passively sit by while others suffer.

Bodhichitta lives through us as a creative vitality that is enthusiastic and energetic in its engagement with life, not just withdrawing and detaching into a passive introversion. Yes, Buddhist practice is introspective and requires that we look inwardly at the state of our mind. Our intention, however, is to be more readily able to act skillfully for the welfare of others. When we tame and pacify our own inner turmoil, we can respond to others with greater care and compassion as well as greater clarity and wisdom.

The combination of deep compassion combined with a dynamic intention leads to what the Dalai Lama once described as a sense of universal responsibility.[23] We are living in a time of global communication and global awareness in which it is no longer possible to live in isolated circumstances unaware of the suffering going on in the world. Once relatively isolated, Buddhism has now emerged into the world, which inevitably means that we must also hold some responsibility in relation to world affairs. We cannot close our eyes to the issues arising within the social and political world. This means as Buddhists we must face realities and practical challenges that are by no means simple to answer.

The ethical questions of such things as global markets, ecological threats, terrorism, AIDS, abortion, and so on all impinge upon our lives in ways that cannot simply be ignored. If the bodhisattva's life is to be an expression of the intention to work for the welfare of others, then these questions may need to be addressed either personally or collectively. We will have to combine the relatively introverted path of personal meditation practice with the need to turn outwards and face the needs of the world.

The Dalai Lama once said that one thing that Buddhists might learn from the Christian world is to be more active in pursuing social justice. He was impressed by what he saw of Christian efforts towards children in need, the poor and homeless, and towards international aid. While in the West we may not have fully integrated Buddhism into our culture at this time, as we do so, an attitude of engaged "universal responsibility" will also be an important and significant aspect of the expression of bodhichitta in the world.

Bodhichitta and a Sense of Purpose

I have spoken of bodhichitta as a source of meaning and as a dynamic responsibility. Both of these descriptions relate to the idea of what our sense of purpose in life might be. Many people seem to lack a sense of purpose in life. This can be in part because we have lost our relationship to a sense of our place in community. In the past, when people lived in more clearly defined communities like the tribe or village, they would grow up to have a clearer sense of their place and what they could offer their community. Whether it was as the local blacksmith, the merchant, the priest, the healer, the midwife, the carpenter, and so on, there was a clear sense of one's place in the local community. This would have given an awareness of one's value in the community and a clear sense of purpose in life. Today, we seldom have such a clear recognition of our role in the community. Our place in the world and in this respect our sense of purpose is largely lost. If I work in the local car factory or at a checkout in the local supermarket, it is unlikely to provide the sense of purpose I am referring to. The idea that we can find purpose in gaining wealth or in becoming a celebrity is mostly an indication of how lost many of us are. Perhaps one of the problems of our time is that there is no natural process whereby we find or are given a sense of purpose within our community.

What then is our relationship to the community at large and what is the role and purpose we might discover in relation to it? What can we offer the good of the community that is beneficial and meaningful? Bodhichitta asks us to look at our relationship to community in a broader sense, as we no longer live in close-knit community. This requires us to reflect upon our particular personal gifts and qualities. This does not mean that in the process of spiritual life we have to find some spiritual gift that makes us special. Rather, it means recognizing how we are able to serve others within the frame of our human capacity. It is our own individual talents and our own personality that are the vehicles for bodhichitta to be expressed in the global community as much as the local village. Bodhichitta brings together an understanding of what we personally have to offer and what we may be called to offer as we dedicate our lives to serve those who inhabit the planet with us.

The purpose found within bodhichitta therefore comes on two levels. On the level of our relationship to the world around us, it is the purpose we find in serving others through our own particular talents and abilities. On a deeper, more interior level, it is the purpose found in recognizing that part of our task in life is to actualize our innate potential. This sense of purpose arises from an understanding of our human potential that is rooted in our intrinsic buddha nature, which can be actualized in this life and lives to come. Once we recognize these two levels, bodhichitta can give a sense of purpose that becomes a steady force through our life. We understand that we have what is sometimes called in Buddhism the "precious human rebirth" and that its greatest purpose is to actualize our buddha nature.

Bodhichitta and Individuation

In *The Wisdom of Imperfection* I attempted to explore the bodhisattva's journey of individuation from a psychological viewpoint, through which individuation becomes intrinsically bound up with the qualities of bodhichitta. While individuation will not at first be consciously oriented to the wholeness implied in bodhichitta, once the process becomes more conscious, the two are intimately connected. In my own experience, once we align our natural sense of individuation with the experience of bodhichitta, they become of one nature. Individuation need not imply buddhahood as the goal, but in the bodhisattva's life, this becomes so. If, however, we consider bodhichitta as an unfolding movement of individuation, then the goal is less important than the fact of its unfolding.

When I introduce the theme of bodhichitta in the context of teaching, people sometimes express the feeling that there is more immediacy to the notion of becoming whole within our human condition than in more abstract notions of buddhahood. This perception need not detract from a sense that the underlying intention is in the direction of buddhahood. However, questions may arise, such as, How is buddhahood as a notion of perfection relevant to me as a goal right now? Doesn't this just become a kind of idealistic or intellectual abstraction that actually blocks some aspect of being present? Is there not the danger of, as they say in the Zen tradition, making where you are going more important than where you are?

When we consider bodhichitta as an undercurrent beneath the process of individuation, it does not have to become too mechanically preoccupied by the goal of buddhahood. Indeed, it may be detrimental to the process to do so. A preoccupation with this goal could too easily lead us to be caught in striving and lose the capacity to be truly present. To paraphrase Chögyam Trungpa, trying to become a buddha actually blocks us from the very things we aspire to. We can become so bound up in an ambition to achieve an eventual goal that we fail to recognize that it is in the present that we open to the true nature of reality. It is in the present that the bodhisattva responds to, cares about, and wishes to serve sentient beings.

Whether buddhahood is consciously held as the goal or not, bodhichitta informs and colors the entire process of individuation. Individuation is the natural movement towards wholeness and a time when we can truly manifest our innate potential. Bodhichitta is the awakening of this process and leads us beyond ego-centered individualism. As we awaken to our potential wholeness, what is it that we can contribute to the welfare of others? Within the context of individuation, bodhichitta requires that we gradually manifest our innate buddha potential to be able to do this. It is this alignment with a natural inner process that makes the bodhisattva's life a powerful expression of individuation.

CHAPTER THREE

The Cultivation of Bodhichitta

Traditional Approaches

WHEN I FIRST BEGAN to consider the qualities of bodhichitta, it was easy to think that this was something I had little or no capacity to cultivate. I felt far too self-preoccupied and caught up in my own emotional problems for the development of bodhichitta to be possible. It became important for me to start to realize that bodhichitta is a natural potential within all of us; it just has to be given the right conditions to grow. We all have the capacity to care for others, even if at first this tends to relate only to those we are close to. We also have some capacity to consider the welfare of others, even if it is limited by our personal difficulties.

We may look at the conditions that enable this extraordinary quality to emerge from two different viewpoints. First, I think it is helpful to turn briefly to the traditional approaches to the cultivation of bodhichitta. Then, I will explore the stages of meditation in what is sometimes called "exchanging self with others," and within that framework, explore some of the psychological implications and difficulties that can emerge as we practice.

The two main traditions for the cultivation of bodhichitta both originated from Shakyamuni Buddha. One passed to Maitreya and then to Asanga, and thence through many gurus to Atisha; the other, to Manjushri and thence to Nagarjuna, Shantideva, and also, finally, to Atisha.[24] These lineages may be practiced separately, in which case the first is known as the "six causes and one effect":

1. Equanimity
2. Remembering all beings as our mother
3. Remembering and repaying their kindness
4. Generating love
5. Generating compassion
6. The supreme intention
7. Bodhichitta

The second process of practice, "exchanging self with others," brings the two lineages together, and the result is said to be more powerful. This process is known as the eleven rounds of contemplation for the development of bodhichitta, and is as follows:

1. Equanimity
2. Recognition of all beings as our mother
3. Remembering their kindness
4. Repaying their kindness
5. Equalizing self and others
6. The faults of self-cherishing
7. The virtues of cherishing others
8. Exchanging self with others
9. Giving and taking (tonglen)
10. The supreme wish / The great will
11. The generation of bodhichitta

According to Geshe Rabten, "Bodhichitta is a development of the mind brought about by gradual change. It is not something which one acquires instantly. If we want to build a house we must first level the ground, collect all the different materials, put them in order, and then begin the construction work—it is a process."[25]

The eleven stages of this approach are usually seen as specific meditation practices so that each stage of meditation builds on the one before. The intention of these sequential meditations is to gradually develop the quality of equanimity, leading to cherishing others and then to the cultivation of love and compassion. On the basis of this love and compassion a form of intention sometimes called the

Great Will arises, which leads to the emergence of bodhichitta and its developing stages.

In the process of teaching these meditations over the years I have become very aware of the effect they have and the kind of psychological issues they provoke. In the Tibetan tradition, two styles of meditation are considered, one called *je gom* or reflective meditation, the other known as *jo gom* or placement meditation. When meditating upon different stages of the cultivation of bodhichitta, both of these types of meditation are used. In the meditations I have included here at the end of later chapters, the approach is to spend some time reflecting on the aspects of the meditation and how they might be relevant to one's own experience. This can be done paragraph by paragraph. Finally, I will make the point that this needs to be followed by a period of resting upon the quality of felt experience that remains after reflection. This will shift the emphasis from reflection to a feeling tone, which is the primary intention of practice.

The feelings these meditations generate may not always be comfortable and may need some degree of exploration. One thing that has become apparent for me in going through this meditation process time and again is that in each of these stages, we are likely to encounter different aspects of our personal wounding and will need to address them and enable some sort of transformation or healing to take place in order to move forward. However, this is the point of these practices. Only once we actually uncover the various psychological patterns and problems that prevent a particular quality from arising will we genuinely cultivate the rounded nature of bodhichitta.

CHAPTER FOUR

Preparing the Ground

~~~~~~~~~~~~~~~ ⌒◇◇⌒ ~~~~~~~~~~~~~~~

Healing Self-Value

WHEN I FIRST BEGAN to study and practice these meditations, I became painfully aware that I was struggling with one particular expression the Tibetans use which is that "all suffering arises from *self-cherishing*" and that "happiness arises from *cherishing others*." I was being asked to abandon "self-cherishing" because it was considered to be not just the cause of my suffering, but almost synonymous with evil. When I first heard this, rather than feeling liberated by the thought, I felt even more distressed and confused. I did not cherish myself at all; in fact, I actively disliked myself. I had terribly low self-esteem and felt I was being told that to actually think about myself, cherish myself, and care for myself was the cause of all suffering. This conflict began to make me feel even worse about myself.

At that time, in my twenties, something I desperately needed to heal was my lack of self-worth. I had also grown up with a sense that to consider myself and my needs was wrong and selfish. As a result, I tended to be unhealthily self-negating and would often feel guilty if I thought of myself. I felt I actually needed to begin to feel positively about myself and appreciate and value myself—to cherish myself rather than give up cherishing myself. As I began to hear these teachings on the downfalls of self-cherishing, I felt that this wounding was being reinforced rather than healed.

As my understanding of both the dharma and Western psychology has grown, what I now believe is that the word "cherish" is somewhat misleading. From a psychological viewpoint, what this refers to is a kind of self-preoccupation that tends to dominate our life and which often comes from a wounded sense of identity. When we lack a sense of self-value, self-love, and self-acceptance, this self-preoccupation can be particularly extreme. Those who are emotionally damaged in this way may not be fully aware of its effect, but deep within they will have a constant need to feel loved and accepted.

If we suffer this kind of emotional wounding, we will cultivate many habits and strategies to try to get what we need, yet so often cause ourselves even more misery. We may mask our pain through a defense that never gives in to "weak neediness" or through a self-negating compulsion to please and take care of others to feel valid. Our wounding may also lead to a kind of depressive self-preoccupation that is hard to disguise. Superficially, we may be tempted to judge this self-preoccupation, but if we see it with compassion, it is simply a reflection of just how damaged we are.

A woman I once saw in psychotherapy came to me because she was distressed by how difficult it was for her to feel a genuine sense of compassion towards the people she met. She ran a small residential center, and her work required that she listen to people's difficulties. Rather than being sympathetic to their needs, she would often feel intolerant and irritated. Her distress was compounded by the feeling that as a Buddhist, she was supposed to be caring and sympathetic. As we began to explore more deeply some of the underlying aspects of her own psychological experience, it became apparent that she would not tolerate her own vulnerabilities and needs. As a child she grew up in a harsh and intolerant environment where there was no room for her to express her needs without feeling judged and criticized. Feelings and needs were unacceptable. She grew to harden herself to her own inner life. This manifested as a kind of intolerant abandonment of what might be seen as her inner child, the younger part of herself as a little girl. When she envisaged this wounded, unhappy side of herself, she felt a kind of loathing towards it. She was in great inner conflict as she split off from her own needs. The result was that she continued to be dominated by feelings that beneath a mask of competence, she was bad, weak, nasty, and unacceptable.

While this inner wounding was perpetuated it would be extremely difficult to have compassion for those she encountered who expressed their distress and needs. Only as she began to make friends with the previously disliked, vulnerable side of herself did it become possible to soften her sense of self-dislike. This was aided by a therapeutic setting that did not judge or condemn her for her emotional needs as her family had. Gradually, she was able to respond to those she worked with from a more genuinely caring, less judgmental place, and to feel less inner recrimination.

The psychological term for this emotional wounding is the "narcissistic wound," and so long as we are wounded in this way, it will be very hard to turn our attention to others. We are in too great a distress in ourselves. Psychologically, this disposition needs help so that a sense of self-value and self-acceptance can grow. Without it, there is actually very little possibility of successfully developing the stages of bodhichitta.

From a psychotherapeutic point of view, what is often needed is the presence of someone who helps us reconnect to the pain of our wounding and holds us with a quality of love and compassion as we do so. It is rather like being reparented by someone who cares for us and can reflect back to us a real sense of our value. We can then begin to let go of the solidity of our negative sense of self and have some compassion for ourselves. This in turn begins to soften and loosen some of the self-preoccupation.

I experienced this very deeply on one occasion when I was living in a community in the north of England in my late twenties. Following the breakup of a relationship, I had gone through a period in which I felt very negative about myself. Feelings of self-loathing and lack of worth constantly attacked me from within like a host of demons. One day, feeling very depressed and dejected, I was walking through a large workshop area of the grounds in which we lived when my teacher Lama Yeshe suddenly appeared. He was alone and walked up to me and with great sensitivity asked me how I was. I could tell he was genuinely concerned and this had the effect of cracking something open in me. I burst into tears and said I felt terrible. He immediately gave me a big hug, which was exactly what

I needed. The sense of total acceptance and love I felt from him profoundly affected me.

While we are still bound by a deeply wounded sense of self that feels unloved, not good enough, and unacceptable, the teachings on bodhichitta are likely to fall on barren ground. Sometimes, as I felt myself, they may even compound feeling bad about ourselves for being "so selfish." We are given the message that we have to give up selfishness, but in my experience as a psychotherapist it has become clear that it is hard to give up selfishness until we have felt truly valued and loved. Those who have been deeply loved and nurtured as children will often find it much easier to feel an inner richness that is able to give to others. The beginning of the process of cultivating bodhichitta may therefore be more concerned with cultivating love, compassion, and acceptance towards ourselves to heal our sense of self-value before we fully take on what it means to cherish others.

Approaches to Healing

So far, I have elucidated a therapeutic view of what might heal our sense of self-value. Another path to healing is through meditation practice, which offers many useful approaches. The practice known as *metta* or loving-kindness can offer one approach. With this meditation, one may visualize oneself as if separate and in front of oneself and spend time sending out a quality of loving-kindness to heal habitual negative attitudes. This can be done by visualizing oneself as a child if, as in the case of the woman I spoke of above, there is a particularly negative attitude towards this aspect of ourselves. I have used a slightly different approach to this within the context of the *tonglen* (taking and giving) practice I discuss in Chapter 10. Here, I would visualize an image of myself, perhaps as a child, and again consider taking on my suffering and sending out happiness. This can be done by visualizing taking on the suffering of childhood wounds in the form of grey smoke and sending out happiness in the form of white light.

I have always felt that the visualization of Chenrezig, the Buddha of compassion, as a loving parent is very helpful in this healing process. In some *sadhanas* or methods of practice there is a description of Chenrezig having "narrow compassionate eyes like a loving parent for his only child." Chenrezig sees us like the loving parent some part of us may still desperately need. You can visualize Chenrezig in space in front of you and then, reflecting on his total unconditional compassion and acceptance, imagine a light of loving-kindness and compassion radiating down into you. Reciting the mantra of Chenrezig can also support this process as your whole body is filled with the light energy of love and acceptance.

A meditation that I have always found very powerful connects to the practice of simple present awareness. We need to begin to soften the intensity with which we contract around our negative emotional self-beliefs. We tend to cling to our self-beliefs in a way that tightens them into a fixed, solid sense of self the Tibetans call *dak dzin* or ego-grasping. From this contracted place, we then respond to events and experiences with the usual range of emotional reactions. If we can loosen or soften this contraction around our wounded identity, it will enable an increased sense of ease and acceptance in how we inhabit our sense of self.

To soften our negative self-beliefs, we can combine two important ingredients. The first is a sense of compassion that accepts and allows us to be who we are, with our flaws and our abilities. The second is a softening and opening of the inner contraction around the solid sense of self. What follows is a simple example of this kind of meditation.

Self-Acceptance Meditation

Sit in your normal meditation posture and place the attention upon the natural rising and falling of the breath. In this process, allow particular attention to the quality of the out-breath as a relaxing, releasing, settling breath. This will enable you to gradually settle awareness more deeply into the body and increase the sense of spaciousness and ease.

Continue with this relaxing, releasing breath awareness for some minutes, paying particular attention to the felt sense of becoming more open and spacious with each breath. Let the out-breath be a quality of ease in yourself as you settle into and make friends with yourself.

After some minutes, introduce into this quiet awareness a notion of acceptance and compassion. This can be done simply by introducing the word "acceptance" without disturbing the mind's quiet clarity, as if this word is a fish that swims through water. Continue with the breath. Try to maintain the sense that whatever attributes and failings you may have, this is deeply acceptable.

If this enables a more soft sense of ease in being present with yourself, then remain with that feeling and allow it to penetrate deeply.

If negative feelings or thoughts about yourself arise, try to just let them be without contracting into them. Instead, let the out-breath enable a kind of letting free. Continue the process of releasing and opening with the breath and the sense of acceptance for as long as you need.

Gradually allow yourself to settle into a quiet, present quality of awareness that is profoundly at ease with yourself and deeply settled into your body.

* * *

The intention of this meditation is not to introduce a concept of acceptance on merely an intellectual level. Rather, it is to use the briefest of concepts to penetrate on a deeply felt level and open up a new potential for felt experience. If negative feelings arise, then the point is to simply remain present with these, witnessing them without judgment, without pushing them away or grasping at them. Then we introduce a sense of total acceptance of what is, without analysis.

Something important to recognize in this process is that I am not suggesting that we replace negative self-beliefs with positive ones, or even superimpose positive beliefs upon negative ones. This can be just another kind of illusion. Acceptance is the beginning of allowing ourselves to be as we are. In time, this meditation can bring about a more spacious sense of inner peace that does not require us to be perfect or free of problems. On the basis of this experience, we may more easily move on to the next meditation.

CHAPTER FIVE

Equanimity

How can I develop compassion if my mind is caught up with all kinds of judgments and prejudices about others? Preparing the ground for the gradual cultivation of loving-kindness and compassion requires that we move beyond the tendency to be biased and partial in our view of others. So long as we are, this attitude will prevent us from genuinely responding with care and concern. We will inevitably be drawn to care for those we are close to and not for those we harbor some kind of dislike towards. To begin to recognize and take responsibility for this bias in our relationships can eventually lead to a more balanced, even-minded regard for others in our interactions, even though some people may be hard to relate to. In the eleven stages for the development of bodhichitta, the meditation that leads to this experience is known as "equanimity."

In the Tibetan teachings of *lojong* or thought training, there is a constant reminder that those who harm us, treat us with disrespect, or criticize us are our greatest friends because they contribute most to our growth. We learn most about ourselves from them and they show us where we need to cultivate patience, understanding, and compassion. To follow such a teaching requires that we change our perspective of others deeply. It requires that we really address what gives rise to such bias.

Within the process of developing bodhichitta, the stage that addresses this problem is actually the first of the eleven stages, although because of what I have written in the previous chapter, I am suggesting that there is something that has to be addressed even earlier. Once we have looked more deeply at our own wounding and the causes for our own suffering, we can begin the next phase, which is the cultivation of equanimity.

The Traditional Approach

Traditionally, equanimity is taught as a way to equalize friend, enemy, and stranger so that we no longer have an attitude that negatively discriminates one from another. This is intended to prepare the ground, like leveling the soil before planting. Loving-kindness and compassion can only grow in a mind that is no longer caught up in the kind of discrimination created by the division of others into those we are attached to, those we are averse to, and those we ignore. The aim of this meditation is to clarify that while we like to attribute blame or attraction to those outside, we cannot overlook that these tendencies largely come from our state of mind.

The traditional approaches to this meditation often orientate around four primary ways of reflecting upon the nature of enemy, friend, and stranger. The first way is to reflect that the status of the enemy, friend, or stranger is not definite. It is not a permanent distinction throughout different lives or even in this life. In *The Essential Nectar*, Yeshe Tsondu writes:

> Also, although now all these migrating beings
> Appear as friends, foes or neutral, and being attached
> To this, I develop attachment for friends,
> Hatred for foes, and for neutral folk, unconcern
> Still, those who seem to be enemies at present
> Have in the past been my mothers many times
> They've helped me in such ways as feeding me with their milk
> And lovingly nursing, and guarded me from all harm.
> All those who seem to be friends at present, too,
> Have in the past been the clearest of enemies—
> Numerous times they have killed or beaten me,
> And even devoured me alive. This also is taught.
> Also those who seem to be neutral at present

In many former lives have variously
Been friends and foes—they've done me harm in anger,
And also, infinite times, done me good with love.[26]

The second way is to examine the state of mind that sees someone as enemy, friend, or stranger. Our discrimination is based upon our attachment to self—its happiness and freedom from suffering. The third way is to develop an understanding of emptiness. Here, one reflects that the label "enemy" or "friend" is not inherently existent as a quality of the person. When we investigate, it cannot be found within the person. The fourth way is to reflect upon how we actually benefit from the enemy, or need to be cautious of the friend because of how they affect us.

THE ENEMY

On the basis of these four elements, the meditation begins with visualizing those we see as "enemies" in the space before us. The term "enemy" can obviously cover a multitude of possibilities, including those we dislike, fear, or feel repulsion, hatred, or jealousy towards. Once they are placed before us, we begin to reflect on a number of factors. They are enemies because we single them out in this way. It is our ego that labels them as such because of our aversion, and within the Tibetan tradition, aversion is defined as the mind that exaggerates the negative attributes of an object and then seeks to reject it or push it away. However, these "enemies" are not inherently the enemy, as this perception is based on our distorted view. Because of our attachment to self and our happiness, we react to anyone that threatens it with aversion. Because of our attachment to the body or possessions, we see those who harm us or damage our possessions and our security as enemies. They have also not always been an enemy. In previous lives they may have been friends, relatives, or even lovers. Even in this life they may have at one time been close to us. Their enemy status is impermanent and not definite.

When this person threatens us, it gives rise to a strong experience of self-grasping which, if we look more closely, shows us our empty nature. The enemy gives us the opportunity to see the emptiness of self as it arises as a vivid feeling of "me." This vivid "me" may feel solid, but when we look more closely it does not have a solid, permanent, inherent nature. Furthermore, when we explore the nature of the object of our aversion with our wisdom eye, so to speak, we see that actually there is no inherent enemy there either. It is illusory, based upon our mind's labeling as such.

We then reflect that the enemy teaches us many things about ourselves. They show us our lack of patience and enable us to practice those qualities that will give rise to our future enlightenment. They show us our faults—our anger, our jealousy, our self-preoccupation—and are therefore our greatest teacher. According to Shantideva,[27] without these people we would not be able to practice the path and attain full awakening. Therefore, they are more precious to us than anything else. According to Lama Zopa Rinpoche in *The Wish-fulfilling Golden Sun*, "The enemy is infinitely more precious than any possession. He is the source of my past, present and future lives' happiness."[28]

THE FRIEND

We then turn to friends and visualize them before us. We consider that those we hold to be friends and want to have close to us become so because of attachment. In the Tibetan tradition, attachment is defined as the mind that exaggerates the qualities of an object and then grasps after it. The friend, therefore, is one who invokes potentially strong feelings of attachment, clinging, and need. It is important to say that this does not imply that all friends will carry this kind of attachment, but that those who do will give rise to a far more complicated, emotionally-charged, and potentially distorted relationship. This meditation is aimed not at stopping us from having friends, but rather at clarifying the basis of our friendship. When friendships are free of some of the effects of clinging and attachment, they can be clearer and less emotionally entangled.

First, we are asked to consider that the friend is not inherently the idealized object we are grasping at. They become friend because of our attachment to self-happiness, which they feed in some way. This attachment labels them as friend, but it will also create a problem for us if for some reason the friend cannot be or do what we need. The friend suddenly changes into something else.

The second reflection is that, indeed, they may not have always been our friend. In this life and in previous lives, they may have been people who have harmed us and have been our enemy. We may have fought with them and they with us. The very thought of them may have filled us with loathing or anger, yet now this has all changed and they are our friends whom we become attached to. Their nature, however, is impermanent and untrustworthy.

If we look at the relationship to friend with our "wisdom eye," we also see that both the self that is attached to the friend and the label "friend" lack inherent substance. The ego that is attached is empty in nature and cannot ultimately be found, as is true of the perceived reality of the friend. There is therefore nothing to hold on to as true and definite in this relationship.

Finally, we can see that the friend is somewhat hazardous. They may cause us to be unwholesome and mislead or misguide us, like the friend who persuades us to have one more drink for the road or who, when I forgot to pay for something in a shop, said "Don't worry, no one will know." Anyone who has some form of addictive tendency will understand this only too well. The friend may influence us to hold attitudes and perform actions that can become increasingly unwholesome. In particular, our speech may become uncontrolled. The friend can cause us to become attached, and attachment will give rise to suffering as much as anger and repulsion do. They are therefore potentially problematic to us as we may become clingy and needy. We should let go of holding the friend with attachment. As Thogme Zangpo says in *The Thirty-seven Practices of All Buddhas' Sons*:

> From staying together with friends who misguide us,
> Our hatred, desires and ignorance grow.
> With little time left to continue our studies,
> We don't think of Dharma; we meditate less.
> Our love and compassion for all sentient beings
> Are lost and forgotten while under their sway.

Sever such ties with misleading companions—
The Sons of the Buddhas all practice this way.[29]

THE STRANGER

We then turn to the stranger—those we have a level of indifference towards. Visualizing them before us, we reflect on their status as strangers. This is based on the premise that the idea of "stranger" is rooted in our ignorance, our capacity to ignore, to overlook. The term for ignorance in Tibetan is *ma rig pa* or literally, "not seeing." The stranger is a stranger because we do not see them for who they are; we do not know them and even ignore them. They do not serve us, we do not need anything from them, and they do not give us anything. Basically, our ego is not fed in any way and so we are indifferent. As with the enemy and friend, we have had many different relationships in previous lives, and they may have been our parent, lover, or enemy. Their status as stranger is not fixed and is merely a label.

Following these three contemplations, we bring these three groups of people together and try to see that there is no reason to discriminate one from the other on the basis of our ego needs and labeling. There are variations on this fundamental approach, but its essential message is that the labeling of friend, enemy, and stranger is based on a false assumption that these are inherent qualities. There is also the recognition that we have to see the dangers in our view arising from what are called the "three poisons" of hatred, desire, and ignorance.

A Psychological Approach

While I have spent many hours using a meditation of this sort, it has become apparent to me that it is also useful for us as Westerners to approach the cultivation of equanimity from a more psychological angle. This is not to exclude the value of the previous approach, but it may add something to our understanding of how the meditation impacts us personally. What I particularly wish to explore is the process of projection of inner emotional material within the context of the equanimity meditation. I am aware that the notion of projection is very familiar to many of us in the West, so much of what I am saying here will be not be new. What may be useful, however, is to see how we can use that understanding of projection within the equanimity meditation to deepen the process that developing equanimity requires. If we consider the nature of projection in this context, we might begin with the premise that equanimity is extremely difficult to cultivate so long as we are unaware of the nature of our shadow and its unconscious projections.

The term "shadow" has its roots in Jung's work, so I think it is useful to consider what he has said about the shadow. Jung believed that a spirituality oriented solely towards ideals of perfection would not address the less positive, darker aspects of the psyche held within the unconscious. In his words, "filling the conscious mind with ideal conceptions is a characteristic feature of Western theosophy, but not the confrontation with the shadow and the world of darkness. One does not become enlightened by imagining figures of light, but by making the darkness conscious. The latter procedure, however, is disagreeable and therefore not popular."[30] Jung asserted that our shadow contains aspects of our emotional and psychological makeup that have been largely driven into the unconscious by necessity. These are aspects of ourselves that we have learned are not acceptable within the context of family, social groups, and wider community. To be accepted, we learn to suppress and hide them within the darkness of the unconscious. There they will remain as unaddressed issues and emotional patterns and reactions that have gone out of sight so that we may be largely unaware of their presence until they erupt into consciousness provoked by some circumstance. The shadow will be held in the dark because we are seldom willing to face it. There it may deepen and darken, as though feeding on the dark. It lives and grows because of our denial.

Our shadow may not be wholly negative. If we have lived in a world where to show feelings of kindness or concern is frowned upon because it is important to be tough, then our shadow will contain these aspects of ourselves. We may have had to hide our vulnerability or our more sensitive side so that it becomes obscured even from ourselves but lives on in our shadow. I used to know a man who was a "Hells Angel" and had grown to be tough and aggressive within the culture of his friends, and to hide any sensitivity or care. One day he showed me that inside his jacket he had a little pet white rat that received all of his buried tenderness and care.

We will begin to know our shadow in two ways. One is through projection; the other is when we are taken over by some strong emotional reaction provoked, as I have said, by outer circumstances. Our shadow is therefore to be found in relation to those we fear, dislike, are repelled or irritated by, or in more extreme cases, hate or despise. I have known a number of people, for example, who absolutely loathe weakness and vulnerability both in themselves and others. A different aspect of the shadow can emerge in what we hold to be positive relationships that bring out our deepest needs, expectations, and attachment. Unlived positive aspects of the shadow may also be projected onto those we admire and become attached to, or are jealous of. I personally find people who are terribly pious and spiritually correct extremely irritating. I guess I have a very pious shadow beneath my irreverent persona. Basically, we can say that our shadow is projected out onto the world and colors it in a way that often obscures and exaggerates reality. Furthermore, we are often totally convinced by our projections such that we really believe what we see to be true.

When we consider the psychological implications of the shadow it enables us to go into more specific personal material that is not immediately obvious simply by considering attachment, aversion, and ignorance. In my own exploration of shadowy material projected onto those I feel aversion towards, for example, I have learned a lot about the complexity of my inner life and the emotional wounds and patterns I suffer from. In my personal relationships, I have seen my less conscious needs and emotional habits reflected back to me in the problems that have arisen. In my reactions to people at different times, I learn to recognize my shadow life. The equanimity meditation enables us to look at all of our relationships and see the underlying material that is evoked by them. It's a rich resource for our personal exploration even if we are very familiar with the psychological principle that is operating.

THE ENEMY

If we consider an approach to equanimity bearing the shadow in mind, again we can first consider the so-called "enemy." Essentially, this is someone who carries, in varying degrees, a negative projection of our unconscious shadow. When we see someone that we dislike or feel repelled by, afraid of, judge harshly, or are prejudiced against, we are seeing reflected a projection of our shadow. When we see someone as a fearful threat and become angry and defensive, we are projecting shadow fears out there. If we find ourselves speaking in an over-reactive and judgmental way about someone, some aspect of our shadow has been evoked in our reaction.

Of course, our shadow is not always so unconscious. Aspects of it do become more known to us. Some of our projections are so blatant and comical that they are only too familiar. They may nevertheless relate to aspects of ourselves that we do not show the world.

For example, I find that "football hooligans," as they are called in the U.K., bring up a strong sense of repulsion towards what I see as gross, crude, often violent, drunken behavior. When I reflect on this, it is clear that I have some investment in being seen as good, refined, and well-behaved and would never allow myself to become so "crude" and "barbaric." I am aware that I may have the potential to be like this but would never allow myself to show it. There is a part of me that is potentially antisocial, crude, and aggressive, but this is buried deep beneath my "civilized" persona and I would not be happy if it was seen. As a result, I can easily project it onto others and potentially judge them for it, which actually blinds me from seeing the real person behind the projection. They become simply stereotypes.

There are certain politicians who give rise to a very strong reaction in me. Some I see as pompous, hypocritical, dishonest, and so on. I can see in my reactions that I am only relating to a kind of caricature, and that I do not see the real person. Can I own that I may have buried within a shadowy aspect of my own nature that could be pompous or hypocritical? Certainly not, and so I project it onto some of those I see in the public eye who behave like this.

Our shadow projections can be gross; they can also be very subtle.

They may be instant, as when someone walks into the office and we take an immediate dislike to them even though we have had little or no connection. They may grow gradually as we interact with and experience difficulties with someone over time. The purpose of the equanimity meditation is for each of us to find those instances where there are reactions that disturb our relationships. From these reactions to others, we grow to understand our own shadowy side more and more consciously. This in turn enables the possibility of increasingly equanimous relationships free of our tendencies to be biased and judgmental.

We may not have enemies in the traditional sense, but may still encounter people and wonder why we have such a strong reaction. Once we see this we can begin to explore the internal process that is so disturbing. These experiences are actually giving us an opportunity to learn something about ourselves that is invaluable. Indeed, in the lojong or "thought training" teachings, we are taught that when someone insults us or treats us badly, we should hold this person as a great treasure because we can learn so much from them about ourselves.[31]

In our meditation we visualize those who give rise to some disturbance or reaction, be it gross or subtle. We then need to spend time tuning in to exactly what our sense is of those individuals. With time, we may be able to name what it is about them that pushes our buttons. We then have two things to look at: our reaction, and the nature of our projection. Can we clearly identify our felt reaction? What are we reacting to? Can we own what we see as something projected from within ourselves? Can we acknowledge to ourselves the negative aspect of ourselves that this brings up?

As we start to recognize our projections, we begin to realize that we are not actually seeing the person as they really are. There may be a hook for our projections to latch on to, but that is not all the person is. We have placed a veneer of our projection onto them and are then reacting to it. When we begin to look behind this veneer, we will start to see that actually this person has their own life. We are, however, largely blind to this. They may be loved and liked by others and valued highly. They may be very aware that they cause others to react and that this is a real distress to them. There is often a struggling, suffering person behind the veneer of my projected aversion and dislike.

A man I know is a typical example of this. I find him extremely irritating and cannot easily spend time with him without ending up in an argument of some sort. While I try to be equanimous and unreactive, he has an extraordinary ability to provoke irritation in me and in others around him. What I can increasingly see, however, is that he is actually struggling with the fact that people seem to dislike him. His defensive bullishness comes from deep insecurities and wounding, and he is clearly very troubled. When I allow myself to recall this, I can begin to let go of my reactions and find a more compassionate place from which to relate to him.

Of course, there are occasions when we are genuinely the victim of others' aggression, violence, abuse, and hostility. We may have been deeply hurt by another's actions. It would be foolish and idealistic to bury the feelings of hurt and deny them for the sake of an attempt at equanimity. This only leaves our wounds to fester. On the other hand, holding feelings of resentment, malice, or hatred towards those who have hurt us will only cause ourselves harm. Harboring such feelings disturbs our mind with a bitterness that can grow like a cancer within. We may live with a sense of victimized negativity for many years.

To resolve deep wounds from abusive relationships, we will often need more than a process of meditation. We may require a period of skillful psychotherapeutic support to enable a gradual release and resolution of trauma. Once this has been done, it may be possible to come to a place of forgiveness and even reconciliation. To gain a sense of equanimity in relation to someone who has been abusive towards us is not easy, but would require eventually recognizing the suffering of the other. This has been possible in places such as South Africa where the "truth and reconciliation" process did enable people to begin to resolve some of their pain and come to a place of resolution. This stands in marked contrast to the bitterness and hostility that remains between the various factions in Northern Ireland.

There is a verse in Shantideva's *Guide* which says we would not become angry at a stick for hitting us, but at the person who is wielding it.[32] In the same way, the person who harms us is like the stick, driven by delusion. People who do harm are driven by something inside. They are often hurting inside. When we come to understand this, it is possible to hold compassion for them.

THE FRIEND

Having explored some of the shadowy responses we have to those who disturb us in a negative way, we can then look to those we feel close to as our friends.

A bond of genuine love, care, and affection may hold friendships together, but what can be less obvious are the unhealthy undercurrents of projected needs and expectations. It may not be apparent that these shadowy aspects are there until something threatens or provokes them. So long as they are unconscious or unrecognized, however, they will distort and confuse our relationships. They can create complications that are often hard to resolve. During the course of therapy I have listened to the stories of the friendships of many people in which something has gone radically wrong. A number of women, for example, described how friendships that seemed deep and loving suddenly became fraught with hurt and betrayal when one or the other did not respond as expected. One of these women saw that her relationship to her friend was based around a mutual need to be something akin to a supportive mother. When she decided she was no longer willing to be in that role because of her own needs, it caused a rift that was hard to repair. Suddenly the relationship lost its warmth and her friend became angry and hurt, as though she had been abandoned and let down. Choosing to consider her own needs rather than always considering those of her friend brought out a huge reservoir of hostility that seemed irresolvable. The friendship seemed broken and irreparable.

In close relationships it is crucial to differentiate between love and need, care and attachment, because it is not always clear. The equanimity meditation may show us where our relationships have become sticky, where a subtle sense of obligation or expectation has crept in, or where a parent/child dynamic exists underneath.

Perhaps these undercurrents become clearer or more apparent when some aspect of our needs or expectations cannot be met, or when we cannot meet the needs of another. Then our friendships can suddenly be filled with anger, hurt, betrayal, disappointment, and so on. If this happens, simply blaming the other does not help—we need to look at our own issues involved.

The question is: do we see them for who they are or are we caught in a view that is greatly colored by our needs and expectations? If we fail to accept our friends as they are, we may struggle with the reality that they have their own needs, they are not always reliable, and they may not be able to be there for us. Similarly, they may be our friends so long as we are a certain way with them. If we change or give a different assertion of who we are, do they react and become hostile? Is there a level of codependency that requires that we stay a certain way and do not challenge the status quo?

So long as our friendships are pervaded by projected needs, expectations, and conditions, our friend can suddenly turn into an enemy. The practice of equanimity leads us to recognize the potential for this as we uncover our tendencies. The projection of our shadow in our friendships means we are not seeing the person for who they are. When we see behind those projections, we can respond in a very different way. We may begin to have a sense of separation and space in the relationship that is less bound by needs and projections. With increasing equanimity, we are able to respond with more understanding, more acceptance, and more love.

THE STRANGER

It is interesting to see that in traditional teachings on equanimity, the stranger is probably given least attention, perhaps because it might be considered that they would give rise to the least reaction. If the enemy reflects our negative shadow projections and the friend exposes some of our less acknowledged needs and expectations, the stranger leaves us with an unknown space that we fill with a plethora of projections. When something or someone is unknown we can project fear, prejudice, and judgment or, alternatively, attraction and intrigue.

Our ignorance of a stranger's personal history and personality means we are unable to do anything other than respond to the immediate signs and signals. We read the signs and go through some kind of evaluation, whether we are conscious of it or not. If we pick up signs that are negative, we will potentially project all manner of prejudices onto them. Imagine a new neighbor moving into the house next door. If we have not yet met, it is interesting to see how our mind looks for clues. What kind of people are they? Their car, clothes, children, the way they behave, their voices, all provide clues to invoke projections onto the unknown. When we enter a room of new people we will be doing this to some degree, even though it may not be particularly conscious. If we keep a watchful eye on our responses, they will tell us much about our capacity or incapacity to remain relatively neutral and open. When I take the train once a week to a place of work, I am aware of a carriage full of strangers, each potentially providing the hooks for projection. If I watch my mind in this situation, it is fascinating what gives rise to potential projection. A red-faced middle-aged man in a grey suit with a laptop, an unshaven, big man with close-cropped hair and tattoos, a young woman with lots of face piercing—all offer a base for potential projection.

I recall the instance of a new neighbor moving into the house next to where I currently live. I wanted to go and say hello as a gesture of neighborliness. Walking up the drive, I encountered a large pickup truck with a group of scruffy-looking builders standing in it, shifting some equipment around. I assumed they were there to do some work on the house. I wondered if the new owner was around and asked where their boss was. A head popped up amongst them with a lion's mane of curly blond hair and a torn tee-shirt beneath, and this man said, "That's me, and I am your new neighbor." It took me a few moments to rethink my assumptions.

The stranger, perhaps even more than the enemy, carries our projections of fear because the stranger is a potential threat to our safe, familiar world. This is often one of the greatest problems with national and racial divides, because while we do not get to know individuals within a different national or ethnic group, they can easily carry our shadow fear projections. This was certainly true during the Cold War when East and West looked across the "iron curtain" and projected similar fears onto each other. Only when there could be a more personal contact between individuals from opposing sides would this fear begin to diminish. Suddenly the feared stranger becomes human and "like us." They also have their abilities and hopes. They also are caring and loving to their friends and families. They have their sadness and grief at losses, their emotional difficulties. They wish to have happiness and to be free of suffering.

The stranger may also evoke positive projections if we immediately find something about them attractive, interesting, new, or different. Within the meditation world, there is a joke about the romance that can suddenly arise in retreat when a participant projects some attraction onto a person he or she has never spoken to. Watching the mind unravel all manner of fantasies about the person can be amusing and, if we are trying to meditate, very distracting.

An encounter with the stranger who evokes our positive projections may result in the formation of friendship and, of course, intimate relationships. Our attraction to certain people because of their looks and the way they dress, behave, and speak are all part of a well-recognized process of encounter that can end in relationship. It is surprising how much of what Jung described as the projection of anima[33] (an inner image of the ideal feminine, usually in men) or animus[34] (an inner image of the ideal masculine, usually in women) is often based upon little more information than a relatively superficial encounter. It is for this reason that I choose to include this within the theme of the stranger rather than the category of the friend. Jung recognized that anima/animus projection leads us to place an inner image or ideal of the feminine or masculine onto a person that then becomes highly charged for us. Without realizing the nature of projection, we can become utterly beguiled or enthralled by the person we are "falling in love" with even though they are still relative strangers. The power of this process is indicative of the power of the psyche to invest inner life onto an outer person. For Jung, because he saw the anima and animus as carrying archetypal qualities, this projection has even more impact upon us. A person becomes a carrier for archetypal forces that are actually an aspect of our own collective unconscious. This means that we are encountering an aspect of our unconscious that is powerful and, one could say, potentially "divine." The projection of anima or animus can give a person a kind of irresistible sparkle as we fall in love.

The projection of deep inner aspects of ourselves onto the stranger in this way leads to a very strong encounter that can draw us into a relationship with "fatal attraction." While this attraction is inevitably tied to projections, it is always interesting or indeed, challenging when we begin to encounter the real person. Much is written in Jungian literature of the process that often has to unfold as we begin to discover the reality of the person behind our projections of anima and animus. It is not my intention, however, to go into this material here, as there are many sources[35] that can offer a deeper understanding. In Buddhist psychology these projections might be considered to be merely attachment—indeed, they fit the definition I gave earlier quite neatly. Jung, however, opened up an entirely different way of seeing the process of attraction based on the projection of powerful archetypal attributes. Understanding this may not be so relevant to the meditations on equanimity, but may be important in understanding why our intimate relationships can be so charged.

Continuing with the meditation around the stranger, there are also those people who, for some reason, we just don't notice. There are times when I meet someone and am acutely aware that we seem to have absolutely nothing in common. I can struggle to make contact, and it is very easy to simply ignore them. Then someone will say, "Did you know he does such and such?" and suddenly I am interested. I have a point of meeting and can begin to open up a different relationship. Until this point, the stranger's life may be impenetrable.

As with enemy and friend, the stranger carries our projections and it is equally valuable to look at our responses. These people also need to be freed from our projected fears and prejudices, our ideals and fantasies that arise from our ignorance about them. As we practice equanimity meditation, we may begin to see the underlying psychological factors that influence our judgments, biases, and prejudices. This equanimity is like the prepared soil in which the seeds of loving-kindness and compassion can grow. While we are still struggling with shadowy reactions and projections, this is hard to cultivate.

Meditation 1: Equanimity meditation

TRADITIONAL FORM

Enemy Begin by bringing your attention back to the natural rising and falling of the breath. Allow time for your awareness to settle.

Once your mind has settled, visualize before you a number of people you might consider to be "enemies"–those you feel strong aversion, anger, or dislike towards. With each person, spend a while getting a feeling of what it is about this person that you react to.

What is it that angers you and threatens your sense of self, or your life? Consider: I see them in this way and feel threatened because of my attachment to a sense of "me." Then think: these people have not always been my enemy. In this life they may have been friends I cared for and enjoyed being with. Now they have become my enemy. In previous lives they have been in a completely different relationship to me. They may have been friends, children, parents, and so on. This current relationship is not definite.

Then reflect: the sense of "me" that is feeling reactive and threatened has no solid substantiality. It is empty of inherent existence. Similarly, the person I see as the enemy, when looked at more deeply, is not inherently "enemy." This is merely a label. Finally, think: this enemy is of great value as my teacher. What is this person teaching me about myself?

Friend Then turn to the friend or friends, visualizing them before you. Think: these people have become friends because of my attachment to my happiness. They feed into that in some way. In what way do they satisfy some attachment? On the basis of this I label them "friend."

Then consider: these people have not always been friends. In this life I may have felt dislike or hatred towards or had no interest in them. Now they have become friend. In previous lives they may have been an enemy I feared or hated. Our relationship in this life is not definite.

Then think: the "me" that is attached to the friend and the friend are both without solid substance; they cannot be ultimately found and are empty in nature.

Finally, think: these friends may also be problematic for me in that they can lead me to create nonvirtue. They may collude with my failings and reinforce what is unwholesome in me. I may need to be more careful in my relationship for this reason.

Stranger Then turn to the stranger and visualize them before you. Think: these are the ones I overlook because of my ignorance. They do not give rise to any kind of attachment, attraction, or aversion. Because of this I label them "stranger."

Then consider: their place as stranger is not definite. In this life they may become friends or enemies. In previous lives they have been in relationships to me where we were close as friends or distant as enemies.

Then once again, consider that the self that sees these people as strangers and the label "stranger" is without inherent substance, being empty in nature.

Finally, place the friend, enemy, and stranger together and allow a sense that there is no true difference. There is no reason to hold onto one as being closer because of my attachment or the other as distant because of my aversion.

Rest for a while with the potential sense of equanimity that remains.

PSYCHOLOGICAL FORM

Enemy Begin by bringing your attention back to the natural rising and falling of the breath. Allow time for your awareness to settle.

Once the mind is settled, bring before you those individuals you feel a strong reaction towards, whether anger, irritation, repulsion, hostility, jealousy, and so on. (Do not choose too many.) Select one of these and spend some time feeling into the reactions you have. Then ask yourself: what is it about them that I react to? Stay with this for a while. Can you see the kind of projection that may be present in this?

Then begin to look at your own emotional response. What does this person evoke emotionally? Can you begin to see the basis of your reactions as some kind of threat to your sense of self? What is that threat? Can you "own" these reactions? Can you see how your projections might live in you as an aspect of your own nature? Can you own this shadow in yourself?

Then think: this person carries my projection of what I most dislike or fear in myself. I do not truly see him/her for who he/she is. I do not see the suffering that goes on in his/her life. I do not recognize the difficulties and problems that are at the root of his/her experience. I do not see how others may value and like this person.

Then ask yourself: why do I judge and condemn this person on the basis of my own fears, reactions, and projections? Stay with the result of this reflection and sense into whether your view of this person is changing. Hold this for a while.

You can then repeat this process with other people or even groups of people.

Friend Then bring before you a number of people for whom you have great affection, where there may be deeper emotional attachments and needs that are a cause for concern. Choose one of these and let yourself feel into what the relationship is like. What are the underlying emotional ties that connect you to this person?

Look honestly into yourself and ask: what do I need or want from this person—what does this person give to my sense of self? We are looking at the shadow side of this relationship, not just the positive —can you own the nature of this shadow?

Then consider: perhaps this person cannot always be this way for you. They cannot always fulfill your needs and expectations; how is this for you? Then ask yourself: what am I putting onto my friend that is a projection of my own needs and expectations that does not respect them for who they are?

If you consider the life of this person, can you get a sense of what his/her life is like with its needs and difficulties? They cannot always be what I need. Ask yourself: can I allow them to be separate and have their own sense of self with their own needs, difficulties, and struggles? Can I let them go rather than expecting them to be what I need? Stay with the result of this exploration and feel into the possible changes in how you see this friend.

You can then repeat this process with other people you have visualized.

Stranger Then bring into the space before you examples of the stranger, where you experience people unknown to you for the first time. Do this with those people around whom you have seen strong stereotypical, prejudicial, or fearful reactions arise. This may be with individuals or groups. Select a few of these and begin to look more deeply into the kinds of projections you make onto the stranger in a variety of situations.

What are your predominant reactions? What sort of projections or judgments do you make?

Then go as deeply as you can into where your projections come from emotionally. Can you begin to own what you see in yourself?

Then consider that you are not seeing the individual person in this process. Begin to consider the life of these so-called strangers, their problems and positive qualities. They are no different from you in wishing to have happiness and be free of suffering.

Spend some time with this process and allow yourself to begin to let go of the projections and become more familiar with the reality of these people. How does that begin to feel?

When you have spent time with this you can also look at your response to those you are indifferent towards—those you ignore or have no interest in responding to or getting closer to. Ask yourself: what is it about these people that I ignore them? Perhaps they have particular characteristics or do not fit into some personal preferences you have.

When you get a clearer sense of this, can you see what the effect of this is? Can you see the way you then respond with indifference so that they are almost invisible to you? Perhaps this means that you barely see them as people and have no sense of the life they may lead.

If you begin to consider the person behind the veil of your indifference, what do you sense? Can you begin to see them as a person with their own qualities and difficulties? How does this change your view of these people? Stay with this for a while.

To conclude, bring these three groups together and reflect for a moment that their different positions are because of my projections and my emotional reactions. Consider: I fail to see them as they are and instead bind them by my aversion, attachment, and fearful ignorance. Can I go beyond these projections and be open to the real person, seeing their intrinsic human value? Try to spend time with the sense of the person behind these projections so that there is greater equality between them.

Remain with the felt experience that is left.

Finally, spend a while reflecting on what you have begun to recognize in yourself that is brought out through this meditation. Can you begin to be more aware of the shadow in you?

Close the meditation with the dedication: Through this meditation practice may I be able to awaken to my full potential in order to bring benefit to every living being without exception to enable them to also awaken to their full potential.

CHAPTER SIX

Finding the Capacity to Care

AFTER WE HAVE leveled the ground with the practice of equanimity, there follows a sequence of three meditations which are often problematic for many of us as Westerners. They are intended to cultivate a quality of connectedness and care towards all beings around us, but, because they are usually based around our relationship to the mother, some people find them difficult to engage with.

The first of these meditations, called "recognizing all beings as having been our mother," is intended to bring a clearer sense of our interconnection with others. However, a simple understanding of global economics and a global marketplace sees the interrelated or interdependent nature of our life on the planet, but it does not imply that there is automatically a concern for others' welfare. This awareness could be seen merely in terms of exploitation of others in a global market. So seeing our intimate interdependence alone is not enough—this recognition needs to be tied to a genuine sense of concern that cherishes the lives of those around us.

The second meditation, "remembering their kindness," is then intended to bring about a sense of holding others dear to us with care and consideration. The term used in Tibetan refers to a cherishing of others that is not the same as love, but implies that we care about, value, and respect the lives of others. This then leads to a reflection in the third meditation, called "repaying their kindness," which is the wish to repay their kindness in a meaningful way.

When I first began to receive these teachings many years ago in Nepal, there was a surprisingly strong reaction from many of those around me. This was principally because we seem to have an ambivalent relationship to the mother in the West. I remember many people saying that they could not engage with the idea of remembering the kindness of the mother because they had had an extremely difficult relationship to their mother. This resulted in huge reaction and resistance to the practice. Some were particularly vocal in saying they hated their mother and would not look at her kindness because they felt they would have to deny how difficult she had been.

If we are to use this sequence of meditations, we will almost certainly find that it will evoke some fundamental issues regarding how we relate to the mother. As a psychotherapist, I am very aware that many people have issues with their own mothers that are unresolved. When I was in Nepal first receiving these teachings, some of these issues came to the surface, but at the time, back in 1973, I do not think we as a group had the psychological understanding to resolve the confusion.

Seeing the same struggle in some of the people to whom I have also taught these practices has led me to a dilemma. Are these practices useful to us? Is there some way in which they can be made useful? Or do we need to rethink the whole approach to the practices? If we consider that the primary intention of these practices is to develop a sense of care and concern for the welfare of all those around us, then we could simply substitute some other kind of relationship that is less emotionally charged, like sister or brother. We could, as some writers have done, consider the general sense of parent rather than mother. What this would not address, however, is that a damaged relationship to our mother has a considerable impact upon our capacity for care, love, and compassion and a host of other issues around relationship that actually need to be faced.

Personally, I don't think these meditations need to be abandoned as unhelpful or impossible for us to use, nor do I think it is always useful to substitute the less charged notion of "parent." We could change mother for some other relationship, but this misses the point that psychologically and emotionally, we all need to resolve the potential wounding in our relationship to the mother. I think, however, that we need to reconsider the way we use these meditations.

We need to reflect upon the significance of the damage to our experience of the mother both personally and collectively. This is not to say everyone has had a bad experience of mothering—there are the "good enough" mothers, to use Winnicott's phrase. This is also not to lay all the blame for our psychological wounding in the lap of our mothers. Our mothers are often the victims of their own experience of poor mothering, and so the lineage is passed on. However, when we look more closely at our collective and individual experience of mothering, we can see that something is amiss.

Western psychology and psychotherapy have for a long time explored and charted the difficulties in our psychological and emotional maturation that come from problems in the infant-mother relationship. To anyone connected to the world of Western psychotherapy, this will be very familiar. In the context of spiritual practice and particularly in Buddhist practice, this aspect of our maturational process is not usually considered. Buddhist psychology tends to orient towards the relatively mature individual with a supposedly "mature" ego development, and there is not really a developmental model. Despite this absence, an exploration of the effects of early experience in infancy and childhood can be extremely valuable if we are to address some of the issues that can emerge as we engage in the practices we are considering here.

The infant-mother relationship and the process of development and maturation is complex, and a vast amount of experience and literature is available. While this is not a place to go into great detail and depth, nevertheless there are some useful points that are worth considering. Many of us must, at some point in our spiritual journey, address the issues associated with the mother and begin to resolve them. The implications of not doing so are quite marked and will be reflected in a variety of ways. We will find that our capacity for close bonds to and intimacy with others will be problematic. Our ability to care and experience empathy may be impaired. We may experience deeply rooted feelings of insecurity and anxiety, despair, and abandonment due to the absence of mother holding. We may experience a sense that our emotional and physical needs can never be met. Our relationship to the body can also be problematic because of early difficulties with a mother's issues around physical connect-edness and intimacy. Our sense of self may be poorly formed such that we are prey to emotional instability and a lack of ego ground. On a broader level, the mother is present in our sense of connect-edness to community and the environment. What Winnicott called mother as "environment-mother"[36] can be impaired. We may experience anxiety, insecurity, and a lack of safety in our environment because of an inner lack of security in mothering. Furthermore, our relationship to the natural environment will be damaged, as we no longer are receptive to its presence as a supporting "great mother." Instead of a healthy relationship to the positive mother, we can have an uncomfortable relationship to what we might call the negative or dark mother. From a Jungian perspective, many of us have a relationship to an archetypal sense of the dark mother that has been powerful in our life. She is the devouring, destructive, poisonous mother that damages our growth into life. She can leave us emotionally crippled and unable to mature psychologically.

In my work as a psychotherapist, many of these ingredients have manifested in a variety of different forms. In one client, her experience of having an emotionally immature and needy mother led to her learning from a very early age to mother her own mother, to the detriment of her capacity to care for herself. She needed to keep her mother happy because if she did not, her mother and therefore her world would fall apart. In the case of another client, the mother was critical and disapproving, leaving the daughter with a consistent sense that she was not good enough. In another example, there was an atmosphere of depression and despair in the mother that became the basis of the son's view of life. In my own life, my mother suffered terrible anxiety, and her persistent response to many of the things I wished to do was a worried "Are you sure?" which left me with a strong sense of self-doubt. Whenever I wanted to do something that involved a challenge, my mother's voice would echo with an anxious sense that I may not be able to do it, I may fail.

If we experience emotional difficulties resulting from our relationship to our mother, this does not imply that she intended to harm us. Rather, it means that her influence over our psychological well-being is considerable and cannot be ignored. The emotional, psychological state of our mother impacts us as we grow up and can penetrate into the core of our being. It is also increasingly recognized in the psychotherapeutic world that this process actually begins in the womb.

To begin to embark upon the three meditation practices I am discussing here, many of us will need to look deeply at the emotional tangles left from our relationship to the mother. For some, this may require actually entering into some form of psychotherapeutic process. For others, it may be sufficient to follow some specific meditations aimed at addressing personal issues and the emotional responses that arise in relation to the mother. In my work of mentoring, I have often found it useful to shape meditations that might help bring about a healing of this relationship. One way that I have found helpful has been utilizing the Tibetan deity practice of Green Tara. With one client in particular I set up a practice that involved visualizing her mother seated before her, then generating the presence of Green Tara in space just above her. I then suggested that, after making a connection to Tara as an archetypal mother that holds the space with a compassionate presence, she spend time looking at the feelings generated by particular aspects of her mother that she found difficult. Letting these feelings be utterly acceptable without judgment, she should then begin to request for Tara to heal the connection. This meant recognizing her own pain as well as gradually looking at the pain and difficulties of her mother. I then suggested that, using the Tara mantra, she visualize a healing light creating a more compassionate and caring space around both her and her mother and in the space between them. A Christian might use an image of the Madonna.

My client went home and practiced this process for several weeks. She found that at first, it was extremely painful and brought out all manner of feelings, from anger to sadness to repulsion and so on. As she continued, she found that this began to lessen and the connection was less charged. Eventually, when she came to see me several weeks later, she said something had really begun to shift. She could hold a connection to her mother that was relatively caring and compassionate, if not yet loving. She began to feel that her own pain had greatly lessened and that her acceptance of her mother's difficulties had a more compassionate feel to it.

If we can begin to heal our relationship to the mother, we will find that the meditations that follow are possible to use in a relatively unchanged form. We may also find that actually doing these meditations helps to bring a deeper sense of appreciation of our own mother and what she gave us. However this process happens, we may come to a place where we find a greater capacity to care for ourselves, those around us, and the planet upon which we live. We can begin to relate to others in a more open, sensitive, and considerate way. We may also have a far deeper sense of our bond with humanity as a whole and feel far more attuned to and connected to the place of community in our lives.

Recognizing All Beings as Having Been Our Mother

For some of us, the meditation "recognizing all beings as our mother" is difficult because it rests upon the notion that we have had countless lives and that in each incarnation, someone has been our mother. The Tibetans consider a number of ways in which we can be born, some of which do not require a mother, such as through moisture or heat. For rebirths in the realm of animals or humans, however, a mother is required. When we were born as a dog, a bug, a fish, or a human, we needed a mother. In the East it is readily accepted that we have had countless previous lives and that the mothers who gave birth to us in those lives are still around, reincarnated in those that we live amongst. We may not recognize them in this life, but nevertheless, they are the countless sentient beings that live around us. In *The Essential Nectar*, Yeshe Tsondu writes:

> Now if we ask is it that in fact
> Every sentient being has been my mother,
> It's because there's no commencement to my births,
> And I've taken bodies infinite in number.
> One may think, if there are infinite sentient beings,

It is not reasonable all could have been my mother.
But it is reasonable, since just as beings are numberless,
So do my rebirths have no finite number.
The reason for this is, there's no first point to be shown
Such that only since then has this mind existed. Thus,
No limit is seen to the bodies I've taken either.
But then, apart from the times I've taken birth
From heat and moisture, or miraculously,
Whatever body I've taken, born from the womb
Or egg, must necessarily have had parents,
So it's logically proven all could have been my parents.[37]

For anyone coming from the East who has grown up with a notion of reincarnation, this idea is very simple. For many of us in the West, this is not the case, and we may struggle to take this meditation seriously. I recall sitting in a café in a highway service station with some friends many years ago. We had ordered a meal and one of these friends ordered a steak. Since I had not been involved in Buddhism for long, I was still somewhat unskillful in the way I spoke about some of its ideas. I recall suddenly saying to this person, "You know, that steak was once your mother." He was greatly amused by the apparent absurdity of what I had said.

One reason many of us will get stuck at this point of the meditation is that we are being asked to seriously consider the idea of rebirth or reincarnation. Since we are familiar with scientific ideas that view consciousness as merely something that emerges from the brain, it is understandable for us to think that consciousness will end when the body dies. From a Buddhist viewpoint, consciousness has its own continuum that is different in nature from the body. Consciousness arises from the "substantial" cause of previous moments of consciousness that continue as an unbroken stream. Our body is a vehicle for this stream of consciousness, in which it will travel for a period and then leave when the body dies, only to enter another at the moment of conception. This ceaseless journey is the cycle of existence.

In the past, I have found to my cost that it is not worth trying to convince anyone that reincarnation is a truth. However, if we seriously consider that the mind or consciousness is not the same as the body, interesting questions arise. We need to ask, where then does it come from and where does it go after death? In Buddhist thinking, the stream of consciousness comes from a previous life-form. We may have no memory of that previous life because the process that takes place between lives, what the Tibetans call the *bardo*, is potentially traumatic. At the time of conception, the experience of the previous life tends to be lost and overwhelmed by the experience of the womb and rebirth. This is not always the case, but it is very difficult to validate what people describe as being past life memories.

There are a few individuals who have some faint recollection of previous lives, but these are usually hidden behind the powerful impact of this life's experience. It is said by Tibetans, however, that in the process of an increasingly deepening meditation practice, some meditators do begin to uncover previous life memories.

The process of reincarnation means that we have had a continuous stream of lives and that the beings we see around us have also had a continuous stream of incarnations. Those we have been related to in these lives are all around us, even though we do not easily recognize the connection. Our previous life connections will not have exclusively been mother to child, but in this meditation it is this relationship to others that is most significant. Potentially, our mother has been closer to us emotionally and physically than most other connections. She is important in all the different states of incarnation, whether human, animal, bird, fish, or insect. As we reflect upon this, we may begin to recognize that all beings, as our mothers, have had a special closeness to us throughout all of our lives. They are our "mother sentient beings."

CHAPTER SEVEN

Remembering Their Kindness

Before our birth we were protected and preciously carried in her womb; we were in a state of total helplessness and complete dependence. Our presence there was not only a great physical burden to her but also a responsibility curtailing her freedom of action. When eating, walking, sitting, or sleeping she was constrained to be mindful of our presence and welfare. This she did joyfully. At birth we give great suffering to our mother and yet she forgets this at once and rejoices as though she had found a precious gem. We have no control of our physical functions, yet she feels no revulsion towards our vomit or excretions, but cares for us gently. When she looks at us and speaks our name she does so in a special way, and her tenderness is not in response to some kindness we have shown her, but is the result of her enormous compassion. She has helped us in countless ways and it is thanks to her kindness that we have received our present stage of development.

THESE WORDS, spoken by the Tibetan lama Geshe Rabten at a teaching in India, show a deep respect and empathy for the kindness of the mother, as he must have felt it. They demonstrate the kind of sensitivity and awareness that characterizes the care of the bodhisattva. What has great impact for me, having met and been taught by Geshe Rabten, is that they were spoken by a man who was once nicknamed by Westerners "the enlightened truck driver."

He was a tough, rugged mountain man who had suffered hardships in his life we can barely imagine, and yet he had a level of kindness and sensitivity that was quite remarkable.

In the eleven stages of meditation, once we connect to the idea that all beings have been our mother, we go on to remember their kindness. While this may be hard for some of us with our history of difficulties with the mother, nevertheless it is a particular way of cultivating a more appreciative and caring attitude towards all those around us.

Geshe Rabten also said,

> As a result of particular karmic relations from the past, there are cases of mothers who maltreat their offspring, but this is the exception and the universal attitude of mother to child is one of love. Since we are attempting to cultivate our minds, we must regard the positive aspects. By dwelling on kindness, our mind develops in such a way that we become able to benefit others. Nothing is gained by contemplating the negative aspects and if we think about the harm other beings do to us.[38]

If we dwell only upon the negative aspects of relationships we have had, it will engender feelings of bitterness, hatred, and a lack of care. I have worked with clients for whom this bitterness has become a deep sickness. While this is not to ignore the harm others may have done to us, it is to suggest that we need to regard those who harm us with compassion and concern rather than with hatred. We could say that whatever harm we receive from others is the result of our own karma, and that they are merely the agent for this karma and will suffer equally for their part in the harm.

Though the stereotypical view of therapy may be seen incorrectly as "blaming the mother" for all our ills, it has become increasingly apparent that this relationship is much more subtle. It does not require the intention of a mother to harm a child, in the womb or soon after birth, for an effect to occur. The mere fact of the interaction between a mother, with her own emotions, positive qualities, and difficulties, and a growing fetus or infant means that there will be an impact. It is this impact that contributes to us developing as a person. As Winnicott implies in his writing, it is not having a perfect or ideal mother that enables us to grow up—indeed, in some respects this would actually be detrimental, as we might never separate from her.[39] It is her imperfections that enable us to gradually grow, separate, and emerge as adults. Our mother is human and has her own problems and stresses, and yet on some level, we place a huge demand and expectation upon her. Jung has written,

> This is the mother-love which is one of the most moving and unforgettable memories of our lives, the mysterious root of all growth and change; the love that means homecoming, shelter and the long silence from which everything begins and in which everything ends…but a sensitive person cannot in all fairness load that enormous burden of meaning responsibility, duty, heaven and hell on to the shoulders of one frail and fallible human being—so deserving of love, indulgence, understanding and forgiveness—who was our mother.[40]

Having become a parent, I feel my view has changed radically. I have more sympathy with exactly how difficult it can be to bring up children and the kind of demands it places upon the parents. Caring for children can be relentless and in many ways has little reward, if that is what the mother wanted.

If we consider the work of psychoanalysts like Freud, Winnicott, Klein, Jung, and others, the tendency that needs to be resolved is a splitting between the positive mother and the negative mother. They recognized that difficulties in this relationship can lead to the mother being either idealized or seen as terrible and destructive. From a childlike place, we may find it hard to resolve this split and begin to hold a middle ground.

The splitting of good and bad mother can have a number of manifestations. One manifestation is that as a child, we may have found it hard to love our mother and have angry, hateful feelings as well.

We have to suppress one and hold to the other. This split can manifest through a child casting one parent as bad and negative while idealizing the other. It can manifest through our needing to keep the mother as good and ideal by making ourselves bad. However we split these two, the division can carry over into adulthood and make relationships very difficult and charged with projections.

As adults, we need to come to the place where we recognize that every person is both positive and negative. The splitting of the good and bad mother leads us to split ourselves, too. We may feel that we are good and acceptable because we split off and bury what may feel bad and unacceptable.

When I consider my own mother, I can see that she was immensely kind to me in caring for me on a material level even though she was emotionally anxious and overconcerned because of her own insecurities. Finding a more balanced picture of my mother required letting go of a relatively immature emotional perspective that was still angry at her for being anxious and needy. It required that I begin to move through the anger to recognize that I could be more adult and responsible and see that she had her problems and actually did the best she could. This enabled me to see that she also had many good qualities that were very nurturing and caring. As I have learned to accept the good and bad in my own mother, this is reflected in how I see others, as well as myself.

From my own experience, the value of these meditations on the mother rests not just on reflecting upon her kindness but also upon her fallibility and human struggle. It was particularly by understanding the cause of my own mother's difficulties that I was able to hold a more compassionate feeling towards her. Through reflecting on what it is like to be a mother and the nature of motherhood, I felt I gradually gained a more balanced perspective. In my own meditations I also needed to include my frustrations, disappointments, irritations, and outrage. I needed to let them be present and gradually let them go, without judging those feelings as wrong or bad. Only by relating to them in a more open and accepting way did I allow them to pass through and reach a quieter, resolved state.

In practice, what this process requires is that we begin our meditation by visualizing our own mother sitting before us, and spend time looking at all the feelings she brings up. We need to let them arise and to witness their nature without pushing them away or becoming caught in them and stirring them up. It may be useful to simply name them or find a phrase or image for them. Holding a place that is free of blame and fundamentally open and compassionate, we allow the feelings to arise and pass. We also need to look at what it is in our mother that evokes these feelings—again, without blame, but really with a greater objectivity and impartiality.

Once we have spent time in this way, we may be able to move to the next phase, which is to reflect upon *her* difficulties and struggles, not with an attitude of blame, but with understanding. Again we need to look at the things about her that "push our buttons," but with a greater understanding of the suffering behind them. She has been the victim of her own background and potentially dysfunctional parenting. Can we see this with some objectivity and understanding rather than blame and criticism? She is someone who has her own life process that also carries its own problems and difficulties. Can we find a place of understanding that begins to see her as a person, not just as a mother?

As we gain a more mature and objective view of her struggles, we can then return to look at the kindness that has come from her as she looked after us. We can remember that if it was not for her, we would not have survived and grown healthily from infancy. We were helpless and she fed us, kept us clean and warm, and did her best to love us.

If we continue in this way, we may be able to actually restore a healthy sense of what is at the heart of motherhood. We may also come to that middle ground that sees ways in which our mother was incredibly selfless and kind in taking care of us, but was perhaps also stressed and troubled at the same time. She may have done the best she could with a great struggle, perhaps because her own mothering was not good either. Once we begin to have this kind of empathic sense of the difficulties and wonder of mothering, we can begin to expand our view out into the world.

Expanding This View throughout the World

In my own reflection on the kindness of the mother, I have also found it extremely helpful to look at the countless mothers that live around me and how they are with their infants. As a parent of young children, I see many mothers who, even though they may have there own difficulties and problems, do the best they can to care for their children and babies. Few of them would intentionally harm their children except through ignorance or in extreme circumstances and when severely tested. The "good enough" mother spoken of in psychological theory[41] is indeed someone we can see around a lot of the time.

In parts of Africa where famine wipes out thousands of children every year, the care, concern, and selflessness one can see in the way mothers look after their dying children is heartbreaking. It is hard for those of us in affluent Western cultures to imagine what it must be like to watch your child slowly dying of starvation, knowing that there is almost nothing you can do. When we look at the tenderness and care shown by these mothers in awful circumstances, it is a reminder of what mothering really demands.

Whether in the human world or the animal kingdom, the consistent care of mothers for their young goes on. Without it, few creatures would survive. Mothers will sacrifice themselves for the welfare of their young threatened by predators. Birds will attack predators hugely bigger than themselves. Tiny animals will hiss and scream at powerful predators attacking their infants. It is a natural instinct for a mother to protect and care for her young. I recall seeing a documentary in which a mother deer had been shot and was dying and still took care of her fawn, licking it to clean it. We can consider how creatures of every kind give their lives to their offspring. This is so much part of the natural world, and yet it is something that can get interrupted in the human world. You seldom see a mother in the natural world that abandons or intentionally harms her offspring. Perhaps we understand this most profoundly if we become mothers or fathers ourselves. The instinct to give up even one's own life for the sake of offspring is so strong. I personally feel that having children has meant more in terms of this meditation than hours sitting in isolated retreat trying to imagine what it is like. I am aware with my own children that when something goes wrong, the instinct to take care and protect is instantaneous.

This meditation begins to soften the heart as we recognize the kindness and care that is so much part of the mother principle. This does not mean that mother has to be some perfect ideal. Her human fallibility is just as much a part of that picture of care. In time, we may be able to hold all beings as a mother would her child. We may also be able to restore a much healthier sense of the quality of the mother.

Recalling Our Interconnectedness

The final part of this meditation brings us back to recalling our interconnectedness. This may be done without considering the mother relationship at all, but to do so adds another emphasis that is very poignant. We begin to recognize our total interdependence and that whatever we enjoy in our life comes through others—through their efforts, their work, their hardships.

It does not necessarily require that others had a specific intention to enable us to enjoy the things of our life. If we think of this in terms of the obvious examples like food and clothing, we can immediately see the global meaning of this contemplation. Our food comes from all over the world (albeit sometimes unnecessarily) and if we consider the people and other creatures involved in its production, picking, packaging, transportation, and selling so that we can enjoy it, the numbers are vast. It is through their labor, their efforts, their struggles that we enjoy what we eat. Often their lives are terribly hard, and to feed a family they must work for very little—yet we enjoy the fruits of their labor. This is something to feel a huge gratitude for.

If we begin to look more closely at our Western life, we can see how much we are dependent upon people in considerably poorer circumstances all over the world for what we consume. What we often don't consider is the impact of this consumption on those who produce it. In this meditation, it can be very useful to spend some time dwelling upon the many examples of this so that we really feel the profound depth of appreciation for our interdependence upon others for our lives. This can counter the tendency to take our good fortune for granted and can open up a sense of gratitude for the kindness of those around. We may find that this can also engender a feeling of guilt for the good fortune we have in relation to those less fortunate. While guilt is not always particularly healthy, in this case perhaps if it does arise, it can be used to increase our awareness of the responsibility we have globally.

Gradually, through a combination of these meditations, we may begin to see the complete interdependent nature of our relationship with the countless other beings around us. We cannot overlook this connectedness to others and the kindness and benefit we have gained through them. When we come to feel this deeply, we will be able to hold others dear and automatically respond to others with a greater sense of care and concern. From this point we can start to move to the next meditation.

CHAPTER EIGHT

Repaying Their Kindness

IN THE previous two aspects of this meditation, we have begun to reflect upon the close interrelationship we have with all those who inhabit the planet with us. Following this, we meditate upon the kindness we receive from them, which begins to generate a sense of gratitude and the feeling of holding all beings as dear to us. Traditionally, the next step is to meditate on repaying their kindness, which usually begins by recalling the suffering nature of the lives of those around us.

Because of the power of media, the lives of others around the world are brought into our awareness more than at any other time in history. Despite this media exposure, we often remain unaware of, or perhaps unwilling to acknowledge, the impact that our Western consumer demand has upon the lives of those who provide what we want. For example, with the increasing movement of the production of manufactured goods to the East, we have little ability to see the working conditions and lives of those who make what we use. Even so, the good fortune we experience through the efforts and suffering of others connects us to their lives in a way that we cannot avoid. All of these people wish to experience happiness and to be free of suffering.

I recently visited a small company that sold building materials because I was trying to find stone paving slabs for steps to our house. I asked the salesman where the stone he was showing me had actually come from. When he said it was India, I asked if he had any idea of the circumstances in which these slabs were produced. He said that he had no idea and it was very apparent that he had never given it any consideration. Having lived in India for many years, I am very aware of how these stone slabs are cut and the conditions of the people who cut them. In the quarries there are both men and women working with little regard for personal safety. Their children are usually present and even working with their parents, and the main hazard to them all is dust. They have very basic tools and seldom if ever have protective masks to prevent this dust from getting into the lungs. Injuries are frequent, they are constantly coughing, and many of the adult men die young of lung disease, leaving a mother with half a dozen children. Their living conditions are also often appalling because their wages are terribly low.

As I was considering these things, I became acutely aware of my interrelationship with those whose suffering is intimately bound up in my life. I realized that I could not simply ignore it. My dilemma was how I might respond to this understanding in a meaningful way. Should I boycott the company that is involved in this kind of trade? Should I make a political point and try to get the company to look at their policy on importing goods from the East? Should I purchase these things anyway because at least it enables people to earn a living and survive? There is no simple solution to the dilemma.

Recognizing our interdependence and taking seriously the impact of our lives upon others can lead to a sense of responsibility. We can begin to consider that we need to respond to that kindness. Repaying the kindness of others, however, is not straightforward. If we cultivate a strong desire to benefit others, we must also ask ourselves, what is the most skillful way to do so? We may have good intentions, but without a clearer sense of what is beneficial, it is possible to actually do more harm than good. This is not to imply that we should simply remain inactive or passive, but that we need to be mindful in how we try to help others.

In my twenties, I was a social worker in a small city that had several particularly poor and deprived housing estates. Part of my work was to keep a watchful eye on a number of families in which there seemed to be danger of children being "at risk." This risk included chronic neglect and the potential for physical or sexual abuse. I

recall one single-mother of two children who was clearly neglecting their welfare and even harming them physically. They had been
abandoned by their mother on many occasions and were severely
emotionally distressed. The social services department decided to
take this woman to court and have the children removed and taken
into care, something that was very common at that time. My role
was to write a report that would be submitted to the court explain-
ing our position. The court case went as planned, and my task then
was to actually physically remove the children from the home and
take them into a children's home as a "place of safety." The most
painful experience of my relatively brief life as a social worker was
removing these children. They began to clutch desperately at their
mother, howling with distress as she screamed at me and a colleague. Taking these four- or five-year-old children "into care" was
so traumatic I wished it had never been done. I still have grave
doubts as to the benefit of this kind of action, and it was one of
the main considerations that made me resign from being a social
worker. I realized I simply did not have the wisdom to know what
was most beneficial. I also realized I was having an impact on the
lives of others that would affect them for life.

Essentially, what we need is a depth of wisdom that enables us to
be clear that the help we give is genuinely beneficial and does not
actually lead to more suffering. We may give money to a beggar in
the street, for example, when we do not know whether or not this
beggar may simply buy another bottle of alcohol and severely damage his liver, leading to a very painful death. We do not necessarily
have the power to see what the consequences of our help may be.

A man who has attended many retreats with me spoke of the
dilemma he has had when, during the course of his work in sustain-
able development, he has travelled to parts of Africa. In relation to
countries and cultures that are so different from our own, where
there are huge fundamental problems of survival, the best way to
help is not at all clear. He may wish to help a group of people he
knows in need of aid, food, water, medicine, and so on, but the aid
that is given may not be what is truly needed. He may go into a

third-world environment with his Western perspective and fail to see the real situation and what is needed to help.

I recall a lama in Bodhgaya, India bringing a bag of coins into the street with the intention of giving them to the dozens of beggars waiting there. The ensuing riot was quelled only by Indian police who, wielding cane batons, ferociously beat back the crowd. This was not the desired result from the practice of generosity towards these beggars, but it was a brutal lesson for me to think again.

From a traditional point of view, it is the recognition of our relative limitations and lack of wisdom that motivates us to go further with our dharma practice in order to be able to be of real, meaningful benefit to others. Clearly, in this respect, being able to help people with their own awakening would be the most beneficial thing to offer. For this we must deepen our own experience. Having a strong desire to repay the kindness of others is in itself a beginning. We must then begin to find some meaningful way to do so. In part, this can be expressed through our work and relationships. Whatever vehicle we use will require that we are skillful and not blind to the impact and consequences of our actions.

In my work as a psychotherapist, this has been very apparent. The aim in helping others in the therapeutic setting is to enable the person to gradually find their own sense of resolution to their life dilemmas. It is not about giving lots of advice and imposing my values and beliefs upon another. This can so easily lead to conflict and confusion when the advice is unclear or inappropriate. If we wish to help others, it may be necessary to let go of the very idea that we know what will help, and instead enter a relationship that respects that the one we wish to help will probably know what is needed. Helping others is often about listening to them and hearing what they need. Too often, going into a situation with the somewhat arrogant belief that we can help is a great mistake. When I was a social worker I think that this was the mistake some of my colleagues and I made. Often, what it created was a culture of dependency on the one hand, and a kind of resentment on the other.

It has also been evident in the therapeutic setting that trying to

make things better or to rescue someone from their pain and suffering seldom helps. When dealing with depression, for example,
it is seldom helpful to try to pull someone out of their distress, or
to try to get them to be positive and look on the bright side. What
helps is someone being present and allowing the pain to be what it
is, held with compassion and love. Our own distress in being with
someone in depression may lead us to attempt to bring them out of
it to relieve our own pain. This rarely helps the other person.

Repaying the kindness of others in the most beneficial way possible is a very individual thing and means that we need to discover
what our particular abilities can make possible. When I returned
from my period of retreat in India, I became very conscious that I
was relatively unemployable, and that if I was to put my experience
into some practical form, I would need to train in some way. For me,
learning to be a psychotherapist was a profound path of discovery
in how best to respond to another's pain and distress. I may have
had a natural disposition, but this had to be developed and refined
so that I became aware of what it truly meant to help someone
psychologically. The fact that I had knowledge of the way the mind
works from a Buddhist perspective did not mean I could apply this
to others. I needed to learn the subtleties of a psychological process.
I am often concerned when I see Buddhist practitioners who may be
very experienced meditators and even teachers, but who are inex-
perienced in how to help others with their psychological process.
Just because someone knows the Buddhist teachings well does not
make them able to be a counsellor or a therapist—this path requires
considerable training and expertise.

The meditation on repaying the kindness of our "mother sentient
beings" is intended to lead us to aspire to develop ourselves further.
Finding the ability to repay this kindness is partly about putting the
welfare of others at the heart of what we do. The spiritual practice
we follow, the work we are engaged in, and the way we relate to
others in our life can then reflect this deepening intention. We do
not have to necessarily change our life radically to begin to bring
this heart to it. We will, however, start to see the interrelationship
with others within what we do as of greater importance. We can

start to deepen our sense of care and our capacity to contribute to community.

Meditation 2: Cultivating the capacity to care

As you do this meditation, try to be aware of the feeling responses that begin to arise, whether they are positive or negative. Try not to judge them or push them away if they are painful or negative feelings. Instead, simply let them be there with a sense of compassion, acceptance, and openness so that they can gradually be released to move through. This in itself can have a progressively healing effect so long as we do not hold on to our beliefs and reactions as though they were solid and permanent. By repeating this process, a gradual clearing of painful negative feelings can begin to occur.

Recognizing all beings as one's mother

Begin by bringing your attention back to the natural rising and falling of the breath. Allow time for your awareness to settle.

Consider that through the process of reincarnation we have had countless lifetimes in which we have been reborn either through the womb or through birth in an egg, and in each of those occasions we have had a mother. If we were born as an insect, bird, fish, animal, or human in previous lifetimes, in each of those lifetimes, someone has given birth to us. We have no idea when this process started, so we have had numberless mothers in previous lifetimes.

So there have been countless sentient beings who have been our mother, and those sentient beings are still continuing in their own process of incarnation. They still exist, incarnating in the beings that are around us, although we don't recognize or see them that way.

Then consider that whenever we encounter another sentient being, at some point in the distant past, this being was closely connected to us as our mother.

Remembering their kindness

Then consider the kindness of our current mother. Before we were born, as she carried us in the womb, we were extremely precious to our mother; in the womb we were in a state of complete dependence upon her and she protected us. Our presence in her womb was often a great physical discomfort or burden to her and a great responsibility, curtailing her freedom of action. In order to protect us in the womb she endured incredible difficulties and hardships. When eating, walking, sitting, sleeping she was constrained to be mindful of our presence in her womb and to consider our welfare. And she probably did this quite gladly, willingly, because we were so important to her. It may not always have been easy for her, but she did the best she could and was glad to do it.

Then at the time of our birth we gave her a huge amount of suffering and pain, but a short while afterwards she had forgotten that because we were so precious to her. She wouldn't reject us because she experienced pain at birth, because we were so important to her. She took care of us as well as she was able.

Then as we grew into a small infant and we had no control over anything, we were completely helpless, all we could do was scream and call out when we were in discomfort and she would respond to that, constantly being aware of our presence, trying to find out what would make us happy and alleviate our suffering. And she would have no revulsion to us vomiting, having filthy diapers, being covered in food, and making a mess because she was happy to take care of us. Without her doing that we wouldn't have survived, because we were completely dependent upon her.

Then in the early weeks, months, years of our life her attention was focused on us. She was constantly alert to how we were and whether we were distressed or in danger, protecting us from harm when we were so helpless. So thanks to her kindness we were able to grow and to survive.

Then consider: as we grew up our mother may not always have been perfect, but she tried in her way to care for us and provide what we needed. She may have had her faults and her emotional problems, but she was there for us as we grew through school and out into the world. We are here because of her kindness. Try to hold a sense of your mother as someone who was both a kind mother doing her best and a mother with failings. She was both a good and bad mother.

If this has been true of our present mother, what about all those countless other mothers? Reflect on all the ways in which animals, birds, and so on protect and care for their young because that is their instinct. They take care of their infant, often at the risk of losing their own life. This we have also experienced countless times.

We can see that these mothers often struggled in taking care of us, they had their own difficulties, but they did what they could and by their kindness, we were able to survive. So the kindness of these sentient beings around us throughout all of our lives has been enormous, just as that of our mother in this life.

REPAYING THEIR KINDNESS

Finally, consider: having received so much kindness from these sentient beings in this life as well as previous lives, if we are to make this life meaningful, then what better meaning than to repay that kindness?

We can also see that their lives are full of suffering, whether it is emotional suffering such as fear, anxiety, and so on, or physical hardship. Consider examples of mothers looking after their children around the world such as in Africa, where children are dying of starvation; their mothers still care for them. They may have nothing for themselves and be starving themselves, and yet they still consider their children first.

Then consider that the most meaningful thing we can do is to repay their kindness by helping them to be free of their suffering and by treating them with care, respect, and consideration whenever we can.

Finish by resting with whatever feeling this meditation leaves and allow that sense of care to grow and stabilize.

Close the meditation with the dedication: Through this meditation practice may I be able to awaken to my full potential in order to bring benefit to every living being without exception to enable them to also awaken to their full potential.

Meditation on the interdependence of oneself with all sentient beings

You can use this second meditation if you find the notion of reincarnation impossible to consider. I would suggest, however, that to use this meditation as an alternative to the previous one on the mother is not so useful, for reasons I have made clear earlier on. This second meditation is a very beneficial approach alongside the previous one. Here we consider the global interdependence of ourselves and all others around us for all that we have in our life. In this respect, it is a particularly appropriate meditation for our time.

Begin by bringing your attention back to the natural rising and falling of the breath. Allow time for your awareness to settle.

Begin by reflecting on the fact that you live on a planet where you are totally interdependent with all of the creatures that surround you. We have tended to live lives in which we isolate and separate ourselves and live in relatively insular, narrow circumstances where we fail to recognize our interdependence. You cannot ignore the fact that everything you do, everything you have, everything you experience arises in relationship to all of those around you and to the planet as well.

So whether it is the food that you eat, the clothes you wear, or the material life you have—you can look at each individual thing and see that they come to you from all over the world. On that basic level, you can see that whatever you have and whatever you do arise because of a global process.

For example, if you buy flowers in a shop, these days they are seldom grown nearby; they are often grown in Africa. Many of your vegetables come from all over the world. Your clothes are seldom made locally; they are made all over the world by people that you will never see. What you are wearing now was probably made by people in India or China. What you eat for lunch today was probably grown by people from many different countries. This means that your relationship to all of these people on the planet is intimately connected. Like a leaf on a huge tree, you are a small part of a vast, interconnected life system.

MEDITATE UPON THEIR KINDNESS

As you remember the interdependence of your relationship to all those around you, you can see the kindness and benefit that you experience from them. You can see that whatever you enjoy in your life comes through the kindness of others. These people put a lot of time, effort, and energy into producing the food that you eat, the clothes that you wear, the things that you enjoy.

Then consider other levels of dependence upon others such as for your education and health, and the kindness of all those who have helped you in your life.

MEDITATE UPON REPAYING THIS KINDNESS

Then consider the quality of life of those people upon whom you depend. Much of the time, many people's lives are in a huge amount of suffering. This may be due to stress and fear, social upheaval, wars and famine, or just living in harsh, impoverished circumstances. Spend a while reflecting upon this from examples you are aware of.

Then consider that as we have this good fortune of a human rebirth endowed with freedom and the conditions to follow a spiritual life, perhaps the most meaningful way to use it is to repay that kindness. Can you begin to hold an attitude of care and concern toward the suffering of all those who are the source of so much of your good fortune?

Finally, stay with whatever feeling this leaves.

Close the meditation with the dedication: Through this meditation practice may I be able to awaken to my full potential in order to bring benefit to every living being without exception to enable them to also awaken to their full potential.

The result of meditation

You may find that the impact of these two meditations feels very different. When I have worked with both meditations in the context of retreats with groups of students, most people had a sense that the first meditation led to a genuine softening of the heart, with a growing quality of care and warmth towards others. The second meditation can give a clear understanding of our interconnectedness in a more cognitive way. This can lead to a stronger sense of responsibility and the recognition that our lives are so intimately intertwined with the lives of others. Some people's response was that they felt a degree of guilt that they were so fortunate in comparison to those in the world whose lives are apparently so much less so. This can be seen as a useful guilt, in that it may provoke a stronger desire to do something about it. This desire may then be expressed on a practical level in the world; it might equally find expression through the process of spiritual practice. This can be seen as why we take the meditation on to the next level, so as to actually cultivate an intention of bodhichitta to be willing to engage in the world for the welfare of others. The guilt becomes the gold of bodhichitta.

CHAPTER NINE

Exchanging Self with Others

ONCE WE HAVE explored the previous meditations aimed at cultivating the quality of care and concern towards all beings, we move
on to a practice known as "exchanging self with others." This practice also focuses on attempting to change the disposition that seeks
one's own personal happiness alone with little concern for the welfare of others. What may be of particular importance in this practice
is the recognition that while we may have an understanding of the
emptiness of self, this does not mean that our spiritual practice has
shifted in orientation away from self-preoccupation. The aim of the
practice of exchanging self with others is to overcome this habitual
tendency.

Having an ego orientates much of our life, behavior, and thinking towards the subjective sense of "me" and me-grasping, or what
is called in Tibetan *dak dzin* or ego-grasping. Our reality becomes
constellated around a subjective sense of self that is held to be a
permanent center of our world. What may not be recognized even
within the Buddhist world is that even if we realize emptiness and
cut through the grasping at a self, the disposition to constellate
everything around a sense of self can still be there. We can realize
emptiness and have quite profound insights into the Buddhist path,
but still be incredibly self-preoccupied.

It has puzzled me when I have encountered someone who clearly
has an insight into the empty nature of the ego or the experience of
no self and yet remains conspicuously self-preoccupied. What particularly surprises me is that they can seem blind to the fact that the

imprint of self-preoccupation is still there, like footprints left in the sand. There is a metaphor often used in Buddhism that if you cut the root of a tree, the tree dies. This can be compared to cutting the root of ignorance. We may have cut the root of the tree, but we are left with a dead tree—it has not disappeared. We may have cut the root of ego-grasping, but the structure of our ego-oriented habits can still remain. To quote Yeshe Tsondu in *The Essential Nectar*:

> If I train well in the three Trainings, as described,
> I shall indeed free myself from the samsaric ocean;
> But striving to free just myself from samsara, not thinking
> About the sentient beings tormented there,
> Is like leaving one's aged mother shut up
> In prison and getting oneself somehow set free:
> Is there anyone less considerate than that?
> Therefore, I must liberate all migrators.[42]

If we consider another metaphor for what I am saying, a ship sailing through the ocean has a momentum oriented in a particular direction, which will continue even when the engines are stopped. Because the disposition is already established, the ship will just keep going. It is the same with the disposition of ego-grasping. Only when it is countered by some other disposition will this change. This is the criticism that the bodhisattva path of Buddhism directs at the path of the *arhat,* who seeks personal liberation alone.

The process of changing our instinctual self-orientation begins with a meditation called "equalizing self with others." Here we are looking again at our relationship to all those we have considered in the previous meditation. Whether we emphasize all sentient beings as having been our mother, or whether we are considering the view of our interdependence, equalizing self with others will be the same.

We begin by reflecting on the nature of our own lives and considering that one of our primary motivations in life is to be free of suffering. Whether it is physical discomfort or freedom from pain, hunger, cold, and so on, we are no different than all those beings around us. Just as I wish to be free of fear, anxiety, insecurity, depression, and sadness, so too do all others. Just as I wish to be free of the problems and conflict, the misfortune and hardship in my life, so too does everyone else. We are not different in this. Since we are all the same in this desire, why do we tend to see our own suffering as more important?

Similarly, we can see that in our lives we are constantly seeking happiness in all that we do. Just as I seek comfort, good food, good company, and nice surroundings, so too does everyone else. In this we are no different. Just as I want to feel loved and cared for, valued and respected, so does everyone else around me. In this also we are no different, so why do I again see my happiness as more important than everyone else's?

In fact, we are completely equal in wishing to be free of suffering and to have happiness in our lives. H.H. the Dalai Lama has a way of putting this, saying, "I am just one and those around me are many; why do I hold my suffering and my happiness as more important?"

Before moving on to the next aspect of this meditation, I think it may be important to consider a kind of anomaly that can appear to contradict what I am saying. Many or most of us grow up to have a sense of ourselves as the subject of our relationship to the world. Our interactions, relationships, thinking, and emotional life express this. However, as I have seen in therapy, there are those who grow up from infancy to be the object of someone else's needs. They learn to see themselves as object.

This dynamic can have a significant influence on how the ego structure then shapes itself. Rather than being the subject who has needs, this person feels that they are the fulfiller of needs. Rather than being the one who is angry, they feel they are the one who is constantly to blame or responsible for another's anger. Rather than being the root of their life, they feel they are constantly at the demand of others' lives.

In those who live this way, there is what looks on the surface like a kind of selflessness, but this is deceptive. There remains an underlying pathology that sacrifices self in an unhealthy way. This person may need to give up the self-denial habit and actually develop a sense of self as subject before coming to the point we are discussing in this chapter. In therapy, I have seen many women, in particular, who need to begin to say, "What do I want as the subject of my life?" This pattern is not present exclusively in women but tends to be predominantly found in women. This is a consideration that was well recognized in the feminist era but still may not have penetrated some aspects of Buddhist understanding.

What we need to recognize is that this is still a kind of self-orientation, albeit a self-negating one. Some of us may know how it feels to be with someone who is totally self-negating in their behavior. They can be frustratingly unwilling to consider themselves or say what they want or need. It remains a very powerful kind of ego-identity, one that is equally self-preoccupied, but in a shadowy way.

We surrender the subject to the other because we need to be loved, valued, looked after, and not abandoned. As Alice Miller writes in *The Drama of Being a Child*, this is a disposition that is often learned very early in childhood in relation to a parent who is extremely needy. In order to survive, the child learns to always be aware of what the parent wants or needs. When the parent is happy, the child can feel safe.[43] For someone who has this experience, the orientation of this meditation may at first be subtly different.

The equalizing self with others meditation aims at gradually opening up the understanding that we are no different in our essential life wish. The one who is self-negating may need to recognize that she is equally valid in relation to others. The one who is self-preoccupied needs to open up to the essential equality of others. Whether we are rich or poor, an important celebrity or a simple peasant farmer, our desire and intention are no different. We may have sophisticated ways of trying to fulfill our desire in the West, but the underlying intention is no different from that of someone in the third world. We all wish to have happiness and to be free of suffering.

Recognizing the Downfalls of Self-Preoccupation

Two primary roots of suffering are considered in Buddhism: one is ego-grasping, the other is self-preoccupation. In earlier translations of the Tibetan, as I have explained, the term most often used is "self-cherishing," which has never felt like a particularly useful translation. I prefer to use the term "self-preoccupation." Lama Tsong-kha-pa in the *Lam Rim* or "graduated path" says that all suffering arises from self-preoccupation and that all happiness comes from cherishing others. While we are caught in self-preoccupation we will act in ways that, either on a gross or subtle level, hurt, disregard, or overlook the concerns and needs of others. We will lack a fundamental consideration of others. With self-preoccupation, the mind becomes disturbed and tight. We easily react with anger, jealousy, greed, and so on. Seldom is the mind happy. We endlessly worry about how we are going to get what we need for ourselves alone.

We may become a meditator, but if this self-preoccupation is present, we can easily become self-absorbed and unable to relate to others. We may cling to our practice and become upset when someone disturbs it in any way. We may only consider what is important to ourselves to continue our practice and have little awareness of the effect this is having upon others we have a close relationship to. It is often shocking to see how even dharma practitioners can be self-preoccupied. I recall when I was in my early years as a Tibetan Buddhist how I would become terribly upset if someone made a noise outside the room I was meditating in. I would sometimes be filled with anger and find it extremely difficult to settle in meditation because my mind was so agitated.

The self-preoccupied mind can become increasingly narrow, fixed, obsessive, and agitated. It is seldom satisfied and creates constant demand. When we don't get what we want, this mind suffers, and when we get what we don't want, this mind suffers.

It is said in many teachings on bodhichitta that this mind is at the root of all of our suffering. Because of selfishness we create endless nonvirtue and, as a result, accumulate negative karma that will bring suffering in this life and the future. In *The Wheel of Sharp Weapons*, a text composed in the tenth century by the Indian yogi Dharmarakshita, this point is made in dramatic terms. He makes it clear that the suffering we experience in this life arises from negative karma accumulated in this and previous lives, all of which arises as a result of the self-preoccupied mind. When we experience misfortune and do not achieve what we wish in our life, this is the result of selfishness. When we experience hostility from others who criticize or are abusive towards us, blaming us for things we feel we have not done, this is the result of our karma accumulated through selfish concern.[44] When we suffer inner discontent, frustration, and disappointment and are constantly unhappy with our lot, this is the result of selfish concerns returning to us. When we experience sickness, harmful interferences, and obstacles to our spiritual practice, these are the result of selfish concern returning upon us.[45] Dharmarakshita then concludes:

> Trample him, trample him, dance on the head
> Of this treacherous concept of selfish concern!
> Tear out the heart of this self-centred butcher
> Who slaughters our chance to gain final release![46]

While this may sound somewhat harsh and it may feel uncomfortable to look at the roots of our suffering and misfortune in this way, it is nevertheless a sharp awakening to the nature of our actions and what motivates us much of the time. Selfishness is endemic in our culture and in certain areas of life, such as in the corporate world, seems to be almost applauded as a virtue. When we look at our own private motives for our actions, we can begin to see just how much of the time we are acting from a self-oriented, selfish place.

When I received teachings on this aspect of the cultivation of bodhichitta, I had one question that troubled me, which was whether there was ever a place for healthy self-concern. In working with clients in psychotherapy, I have also seen the occasions when a healthy self-orientation is needed. Possibly the most important cases in which I have seen this are when someone I have worked with has needed to be more assertive about her needs because to do otherwise was actually leading to a state of ill health. Here we come to a significant consideration, which is that when we have a healthy relationship to our self, there will be times when self-assertion is needed. To allow someone to abuse us and be unable to say no is

unhealthy and usually comes from a previous experience of someone abusing us and our having been unable to do anything about it,
often when we were children.

When we have a poor sense of self we can easily become formless
in the sense that we do not express our boundaries or our "shape"
and may then be taken advantage of to our detriment. I have known
a number of Buddhist friends who had a disposition to be self-effac-
ing and self-negating in a particularly unhealthy and detrimental
way. They would often find themselves being taken advantage of
and feeling powerless to do anything about it. They would tell themselves that they had to give up "self-cherishing" and so let what was
happening continue. I found this very sad and frustrating to watch
because it became increasingly clear that they were struggling inside
with something they had been told was a taboo—looking after
themselves. In the case of these friends, it was clear that their lack
of self-assertion was actually a cause of more suffering. In many
ways, it was actually reinforcing their wounding. It also meant that
those who took advantage were being quite abusive in what they
were doing.

We should not confuse a healthy self-regard and self-assertion
with what is being considered in this meditation. Perhaps we need
to learn to differentiate the two because as I discuss in Chapter 4,
so long as we have a wounded sense of self-value or self-worth, it is
easy to exacerbate our psychological problems and to mistake this
practice with something that actually rewounds us.

Learning to let go of the disposition to be self-preoccupied is not
an easy step to take because it will challenge us where we defensively
still hold on. Once we become aware of the disposition, we will see
it time and again in relatively insignificant as well as in major ways.
I saw this in a small way as I walked to work one morning. I saw a
worm struggling to cross the footpath and in danger of drying up
and dying. I had a moment of choice in which I could have picked
up the worm and placed it in the grass, potentially saving its life.
I didn't, I regret to say, because there were some people coming
towards me and I suddenly felt embarrassed about what they would
think about me.

I experienced this lesson in a larger way when my wife and I moved to a new house. Our neighbors moved in at roughly the same time and soon afterwards applied for permission to build a large extension at the back of the house. Because we had only just moved, we wanted to be relatively easygoing and friendly and so made no objections to the plans. Only later did it begin to dawn on us that this extension was going to overshadow our garden.

As soon as this began to sink in, I could feel the contraction start. "This is going to ruin my house; it will cut out the sun and be a horrible intrusion." I could feel the self-preoccupation grow with quite obsessive thinking and the occasional sleepless night. As I contracted into myself I felt angry, disappointed, resentful, and filled with plans to try to challenge the planning permission they had received. I could see that I had an option to either go into a tight, agitated hell of self-preoccupation, or I could begin giving some space to it and let go. One way would cause me continual distress, while the other could bring relative peace.

Letting go is not the same as doing nothing or letting everyone walk over you. But when we go into the contracted space, it *hurts*. When we let go, there is the possibility of doing something about our situation, but not from the same emotional place. I could, for example, go and discuss the situation with the neighbor, which is what we did eventually do. Before I could do that, I needed to come out of the contracted place because I would just get angry, we would get into locking horns, and it would lead to disaster. Because I wouldn't want to listen to his view about it, there wouldn't be any kind of compromise.

When we have let go of the contracted self-preoccupation, we begin to have a choice. In the example I have given above, I could just say: okay, that's just the way it is, and let it go. There was a part of me that needed to do that. There are many occasions when that is *not* what we should do. We should go forward and say: this is not acceptable, this isn't okay for me. Letting go of self-preoccupation does not imply passivity. It means recognizing that the cause of suffering is the contraction into ourselves in a way that actually increases the pain. When we stay open, we can still assert what is important for us. It requires a certain kind of inner strength to keep our heart open.

In the process of cultivating bodhichitta, here we start to let go of the old habit that is small-, petty-mindedness. We open to a bigger picture that really realizes that these are small things, what's the point of getting so upset about them? If we consider our problems in relation to the terrible events happening in the world, we get them in perspective.

The more awareness we apply to this process in ourselves, the more we will see those times when we could make a choice. We can either contract and tighten, or we can open and give something more space. We can get caught in narrow, limited conceptions about things, or we can open to the bigger picture. The more we recognize this in ourselves, the more it becomes painfully evident that the source of suffering is self-grasping, self-preoccupation, self-contracting. Whether we have an understanding of emptiness or not, we can see that because the habit is instinctual, it will remain unless we address it. This habit needs to be gradually turned around so that we instead begin to open and let go or let be.

Genuine letting go of self comes when we are in a healthier relationship to ourselves, not from a place of pathology. While we are still emotionally wounded, this is very difficult to do. When our sense of self-value is reasonably healthy and stable, we can then start to surrender all those habits that were orientated towards our own self-gratification. We can begin to respond to the needs of others and shift the orientation of our concern.

Recognizing the Benefits of Cherishing Others

Once we have recognized our self-preoccupation, we move to the next aspect of the meditation. Here we start to recognize that the mind that begins to cherish others is more spacious and open, more at peace with itself. It does not become so obsessively caught up in small, petty things that in the larger picture are somewhat insignificant.

Bodhichitta has sometimes been called the "openness mind"[47] and grows as we open to a bigger picture. When we let go and open, we begin to recognize our shared place in the world and the interdependence of our lives. Shantideva reminds us that the suffering of one is the suffering of all.

In the traditional teachings it is often stated that the benefits of cherishing others are threefold. Firstly, if we wish to have happiness in our own life, then cherishing others is what will create its causes. The positive, wholesome actions that arise through cherishing others are the karmic seeds that give rise to all of our happiness in this and future lives. So cherishing others gives us the fortunate conditions to experience our own happiness as a natural by-product. Secondly, if we are considerate and cherishing of others, then we will also experience happier, more fulfilling relationships and a more harmonious life. Thirdly, we will experience a more peaceful and open inner quality of mind because we are no longer caught up in the contracted pain of self-preoccupation.

What is interesting about these benefits is that they are beneficial for ourselves, a kind of enlightened self-interest. Learning to cherish others as more important than ourselves just because we care about them is not an easy process. We will need to learn to change the direction of our normal attention. We will need to begin to give up something of ourselves in a way that is very challenging. This is similar to when a parent comes up against the edges of where she must let go of what she wants and consider what the child needs. Can we begin to give our attention to others and do so with openness and care, without considering what we will receive in return?

As I began to approach the theme of cherishing others, I found that I encountered all my resistances, my blocks, and my inability to surrender the self. As I have suggested earlier, it felt as though I was turning the tide against an instinct that had been there for a long time. This requires the surrender of an old, cherished way. Learning to cherish others can be seen as a kind of self-sacrifice that does not always come in a healthy way. There are ways in which self-sacrifice can come from pathology, when sacrifice is viewed as the only way to gain a sense of self-worth.[48] There are also the compulsive carers who seem unable to live without someone to place in the role of the helpless. There are those who embody a psychological disposition sometimes called the "dependent-endearing"[49] character type, which needs to be liked and wants to please others to feel secure. These tendencies can look as though they are oriented to cherish others on the surface, when beneath the surface they are another form of self-preoccupation.

If we cannot actively start to place the welfare of others as more important than self, then at least we can begin by considering the fact that our actions impinge upon others and that we do not live in a vacuum. When I look more deeply at my own life, I can see that a very simple shift in the thoughtfulness I give in considering others can be very beneficial. Considering others in relation to our actions and intentions can be such an easy thing to do and yet can make a huge difference to the way others experience us. I know from my own experience that when someone asks me how I feel about something they wish to do, then at the very least, I have been considered. Conversely, I am sometimes shocked when someone does something that shows absolutely no consideration. This can be a simple thing such as a builder not turning up to do a job and not notifying me that he cannot make it. It can be someone parking across two parking spaces. There are often relatively small and simple things that reflect a lack of consideration that can be easily rectified if we recall that others are affected by our actions or, for that matter, our inactions. Consideration of others enables a more harmonious sense of community. It makes each person feel that they have a place and are valued rather than disregarded.

The capacity to place others' welfare as more important and actively seek to care for them can naturally grow out of an increased consideration of others. This may not mean seeing others' welfare as more important than our own, necessarily, but it is a move in that direction. Taking this step is something that requires a deep change of relationship to oneself. I have found in my own relationship to my children that my reluctance to let go of self and surrender my needs for their sake is challenged again and again. Sometimes I find I can make the necessary inner step, while at other times I find I struggle to let go of my own needs. Even so, it gives me a glimpse of what the bodhisattva's gift is in being able to surrender self-preoccupation.

As we look more towards the welfare of others, we also need to recognize that we have our own human limitations in terms of what we are actually capable of. When I have introduced this meditation to groups, a number of people have responded by saying that their lives are such that they may cherish others in a context of their work as carers, therapists, and parents, but realize that they also need time for themselves. This may seem a contradiction to the essence of the practice, but it perhaps needs to be placed in context. From my own and others' sense of working in intensive practices such as psychotherapy, there is a limit to the degree of caring for another that is possible without a clear, healthy understanding of our own needs and limitations. Personally, I have found that following intensive periods of therapeutic or teaching work, I need space and time to recharge. This kind of work is exhausting and needs to be placed alongside a healthy recognition of what replenishes our own resources. Endless, unbounded giving of time and energy cannot be sustained, even though we may wish to care for others.

A second point that has emerged through this practice is that there are times when our focus upon some task or creative process can seem to be antithetical to the cherishing of others and may bring a level of conflict. I have found this in my own life when I am engaged in some task that needs to be completed and find that I have a level of focus that is not easily broken. When a child's needs come into conflict with this unfolding process, this is not easy to resolve. Artists, for example, may find they are compelled by some inner need to create that does not easily give way to the demands of those around. This can sound extremely self-centered but may also need to be understood more deeply. Jung recognized that there may be times when what he called the Self,[50] as a deeper seat of intention and wisdom within the psyche, akin to the inner guru or our buddha nature, places a demand upon the ego to follow some inner call that would be unhealthy to block or deny. Indeed, it is often the blocking of this call that can cause psychological ill health. The question may arise, therefore, what if this call runs counter to some other demand to consider the welfare of others? One could say that the Buddha's act of leaving his home and going out on his journey of Self-actualization was an example of this. To do so, he had to leave his wife and child.

As I have discussed at some length in *The Wisdom of Imperfection*, the bodhisattva responds to this Jungian sense of Self through a process of individuation that unfolds in his or her life journey. The power of the Self is sometimes irresistible and it can seem that we are asked to do something that is apparently self-centered. Perhaps it is more appropriate to say, however, that this is Self-centered.

There are inevitably times when we will feel a conflict between the powerful pull of the Self and the immediate response we need to make to those around us. An example of this comes from a woman I have mentored who lives in the U.S. She is a mother of two children who are still at an age that requires consistent presence and care from her. Her husband has a full-time job, which means that he is not always able to take over some of the caring role. Her situation is familiar to many women who have had a sense of personal direction, perhaps through work, and then have to relinquish this to look after young children. In recent years, she has become increasingly involved in Buddhist practice and has a great aspiration to be able to deepen her experience through periods of retreat with her teacher. Since she trained as a yoga teacher and psychotherapist, there is a side of her that is also longing to respond to the inner call to work with others, expressing the part of herself that is brought alive by this process. Her dilemma was that she used to feel constant conflict. When her life became completely occupied with looking after the children, she yearned for the time when she could work again or do retreat, and felt bad about the resentment that arose. When she did create the circumstances to go and spend time with her Buddhist teacher, she felt that she was neglecting her children. The torment this dilemma brought was almost unbearable for her. She was torn between a strong calling to devote at least some of her life to her spiritual path and having to let go of much of this to look after her children.

In part, the resolution to her conflict was to live with the dilemma rather than avoid it. By opening to the conflict, she found the patience to allow her children time to grow, recognizing that they are also part of her spiritual practice. Further resolution came by letting go of some of the ideal of being either the perfect mother or the perfect practitioner. She also began to feel that it was okay for her to find the resources to have some of what she needed for herself without feelings of guilt, while also looking after her children. I am glad to say she seems to have now found a balance that she can live with more comfortably that does not split these two sides of her life.

In my own life, this dilemma is often present as I am drawn to deepen my own Buddhist practice, to write and paint, and yet am conscious that I must let go of some of this to support my family. I feel extremely fortunate that much of the work I do to support my family is also aligned to my spiritual practice. The pull of the Self and the practicalities of life do not have to be at odds with each other, but it will often require a great deal of work to align the two.

For some people, the conflict between the need to look after the welfare of others and the desire to be true to some deep inner calling coming from the Self can be a constant dilemma. An artist may need to respond to the profound urge to paint that comes from deep within even though it may lead to a neglect of personal relationships. It can mean that there may be times when it is almost impossible for someone to not be hurt in some way by our actions. However, seldom can we afford psychologically to give up one for the sake of the other. As I have felt in my own life, I have to find a middle way between the pull of the Self and my need to be responsible in my life for family and work. Holding the tension between these two can potentially bring some kind of resolution, a kind of third position that is inclusive rather than exclusive. Even when we begin to get this right, we still need to be aware of the effect our life has upon others and respond as skillfully as we are able.

Exchanging Self with Others

The concluding aspect of this practice leads to what is usually described as the willingness to exchange self with others. This profound step is a process of mind training that gradually develops through meditation so that there is an inner shift of focus. Rather than remaining self-oriented, we place the other at the center of our awareness. Rather than considering our own happiness, we think of the happiness of the other. Rather than considering our own release from suffering, we consider the release of the other. The thought that is generated is, "May I take on the suffering of the other."

It is this capacity that is being gradually developed in the meditation so that the bodhisattva slowly orientates the whole of his or her being to the welfare of others. In many ways, this attitude may be considered one of the most significant aspects of a bodhisattva's qualities and is also perhaps the most challenging to develop. It requires a constant reminder, in circumstances that will tend to lead us to consider self first, to begin to really consider other first. It is for this reason that there are a number of particularly specialized teachings called lojong or thought transformation.

At the heart of the thought transformation practice is the cultivation of an attitude that virtually replaces self with other as the primary object of attention. Whereas previously all of our thoughts and intentions centered around the self as the subject, the subject of experiences becomes the other. I referred to this when I spoke of those who from a place of pathology will experience themselves as the object to others' subject, rather than being the subject themselves. This time, there is a conscious choosing to shift the focus away from self, but not from a place of pathology. On the basis of a healthy sense of self with the recognition of the value of others, we begin to place the central importance in the other. Gradually, as we practice this service towards others, it becomes second nature, and what was at first something of a struggle becomes completely normal. On the basis of this shift of focus, the next practice, known as *tonglen*, develops the process still further.

Meditation 3: Equalizing and exchanging self with others

Begin by bringing your attention back to the natural rising and falling of the breath. Allow time for your awareness to settle.

As you settle, try to reconnect with the sense of your interconnectedness with all the countless mother sentient beings that inhabit the planet with you. Remember that through countless lifetimes, and in this life in particular, you have had a close connection to them all. Your happiness arises in dependence upon them.

EQUALIZING SELF WITH OTHERS

Reflect on how in this life, one of the things that you are constantly seeking is a way out of suffering. Much of your day-to-day occupation is about finding a way of getting out of suffering. Even the simple things that you do, such as putting on clothes or eating food, are about avoiding suffering.

Then look at all of those around you, whether those you are close to, like relatives and close friends, those who are distant from you, or even the animal kingdom, birds and insects: if you look at their lives, the central occupation is that they seek to be free from suffering. They are no different; they are just like you. All other beings around you seek to be free from pain and suffering and to gain happiness, which is why they do the things that they do.

Just as you seek physical comfort or the freedom from pain, hunger, and cold, in the same way, all these countless beings around us do the same thing. Just as you wish to be free from emotions like fear, depression, anxiety, sadness, it is the same with all those around you; they also wish to be free from these emotions. Just as you wish to be free of problems, of conflicts, of hardships in life, so do all these others. They are no different.

Then ask yourself, "Why do I hold my pain, my suffering, and my hardships as more important when we are all equal in wishing to be free from suffering?"

Then if you look at your life, you are constantly engaged in seeking happiness in what you do, to be free of dissatisfaction. Those around you are no different. Their actions are aimed principally at attaining happiness. Just as you seek comfort, food, pleasant company, nice environments, good friends in order to have happiness, that is what they all would like. Just as you want to feel loved and cared for, valued and respected, so do all these other beings around you. Just as you want to have a good feeling about yourself, to have a sense of self-acceptance and peace with yourself, it is the same with all these others.

So why do you consider your own happiness alone to be more important, when we all have the same wish to be free from suffering and to have happiness? We are no different. We all have the same aspiration, the same intention in life. We may not know how to find happiness and may harm others in the process, but we have the same intention. Remain with this sense of equalizing oneself with others for a while.

There may be a metaphor that comes to mind about your equality with all others–such as a grain of sand on the beach. There isn't one grain of sand that is more important than the others that make up the beach. Or one could think of a blade of grass in the lawn or a tree in the forest.

Downfalls of self-preoccupation

Then we come to the recognition that the source of all of our suffering arises from the mind of self- preoccupation. The Buddha taught that there is no more negative force in the world than self-preoccupation. All of our suffering and the suffering of those around us, the suffering of nations and of the planet as a whole, comes from self-indulgent self-preoccupation.

Being caught up in a kind of narrow self-preoccupation about your life, do you think of just your own happiness at the expense of others? So then when something goes wrong in your day, do you contract into an unhappy space that arises through self-preoccupation, and cling to yourself?

When someone upsets you or does something to make you angry, the inner suffering that you experience comes from self-preoccupation and from holding yourself too tightly, too seriously, too solidly. If you go into a kind of self-pitying victim space about your life, this arises from self-preoccupation, from just thinking of your own happiness. When things don't go the way you want them to, or you can't get what you want, you suffer because of this self-preoccupation. Spend a few minutes looking at your own life to see how this exists in you, where you see yourself getting caught in that internal suffering because of self-preoccupation.

THE BENEFITS OF CHERISHING OTHERS

And then finally, consider the benefits of cherishing others.

If you wish to have both temporal happiness and the potential happiness of full awakening, then this arises from cherishing others. If you see this on the level of just having a much healthier, more caring, friendly kind of interaction with others, it comes from cherishing others. People appreciate it and respond to it positively, and that brings us happiness. So if you want your own happiness as much as the happiness of others, it arises from cherishing others.

If you think on the level of karma, the wholesome actions and the virtue that give rise to positive experience, positive qualities, and your awakening all arise from cherishing others, from considering others' happiness as important. If you want a peaceful mind and an open heart, then this arises from cherishing others.

So when you begin to let go of the tendency to think only of your own happiness, your own self-preoccupation, and open to others, cherish others, then it will change the experience of your day-to-day meeting with others, as you encounter them, and that gives rise to happiness both for yourself and for others.

Finally, rest with whatever feeling remains.

Close the meditation with the dedication: Through this meditation practice may I be able to awaken to my full potential in order to bring benefit to every living being without exception to enable them to also awaken to their full potential.

CHAPTER TEN

The Practice of Tonglen

SOME YEARS AGO, a client of mine who was a very dedicated practicing Christian came to me and said he had been doing a meditation called "tonglen" taught to him by another Christian friend. He felt that it was very profound and gave him a strong sense of the sacrifice Christ had made. He was interested to know where this practice had come from, as he thought it had something to do with Buddhism. Since that time, I have on many occasions heard people describe how they have found a benefit from this practice even though it has been taken somewhat out of context. In the unfolding of bodhichitta, following the process of exchanging self for others, we move more specifically to the cultivation of compassion and loving-kindness in the practice of tonglen.

The practice of tonglen or, from the Tibetan, "taking and giving," combines meditations on the cultivation of both compassion and loving-kindness. The cultivation of what in Sanskrit is known as *maha karuna* or "great compassion" and *maha maitreya* or "great love" can be done separately, but in the practice of tonglen, these two are brought together in a particularly effective way. The Tibetans define these two qualities very clearly. Compassion is the desire that all beings should be free of suffering, and love is the desire that all beings should be endowed with happiness. In the practice of tonglen, these two are placed side by side such that "taking" is a willingness to take away the sufferings of sentient beings, and "giving" is the willingness to give happiness.

Before we embark upon the actual practice of tonglen, however, it would be worth reflecting more deeply upon the qualities of compassion and love. While the definitions I have given above may seem simple, the actual qualities and attributes of compassion and love are somewhat more complex.

Compassion

It is often said that if we have not suffered, it is hard to have compassion. It certainly may be hard to identify with another's suffering if we have not experienced something similar. Compassion may be seen as a collection of qualities with a central disposition that is often described by the Tibetans in the thought, "How wonderful it would be if all beings were free of suffering and the causes of suffering."[51] The compassionate wish that beings become free of suffering is, however, blended by a texture of qualities that are all part of the active expression of compassion. Compassion brings together care, empathy, acceptance, presence, nonjudgment, and other qualities that create a rich blend.

Compassion as a quality of care is like moisture in the atmosphere. It is a feeling environment in which we can live or in which we care for those around us. When compassion is present, it can feel almost tangible, like stepping into the moisture of a tropical greenhouse. When it is absent, the atmosphere can feel dry, arid, and harsh. This moisture does not have to have a specific reference point or focus and so remains just as a general atmosphere. If the need arises, however, compassion can focus and become more like the droplets of rain that fall onto a particular place.

As a therapist, I have felt that the quality of a compassionate environment is vital to a caring process. A therapist may bring all manner of skills and understanding into the therapeutic relationship, but if compassion is missing, a fundamental catalyst for healing is absent. As a parent, I also feel that this is a necessary part of caring for children. When it is lacking, the home environment will often feel harsh and cold. In the therapeutic setting I often hear clients describe how this was the kind of environment they grew up in. The lack of compassion they experienced would often carry with it judgment and criticism that would create a very unsafe environment in which to be vulnerable or express feelings. In the context of the therapeutic process, a client's childhood experience can be felt in the emotional atmosphere they create around themselves. I have sometimes experienced this as a kind of metallic harshness in the room, and when I asked about it, the person related that this was exactly how they experienced one of their parents, particularly mother. When a person with this experience begins to allow the presence of a compassionate holding, they may relax and feel safe for the first time.

As compassion becomes more focused, it needs to carry with it a quality of being nonjudgmental, or what is sometimes called "unconditional compassionate regard." Compassion in this sense is having the ability to receive the other person as they are. When we can let go of the disposition to be judgmental, we are able to allow and accept someone to be as they are without making them feel that they are wrong or bad. If someone is in pain or distress or having strong negative feelings, compassion is able to respond to this with a sense of acceptance that does not judge or condemn it.

When we meet others, if we have a disposition to be judgmental, we will find it very difficult to have genuine contact. Instead, we will find ourselves caught up in projections and reactions that blind us to the reality of the person. We will lack the compassion that allows them to simply be as they are. Once the Dalai Lama was asked how he was able to meet so many people and respond to them all with a similar quality of interest. He said it was because he would always view them with compassion. On the number of occasions I was fortunate enough to meet His Holiness while I was living in India, I always had the sense that he was totally accepting of me without judgment, regardless of my faults and failings.

This does not imply that we overlook what someone may have done or the way someone is being. We do not lose the capacity to discern what is and is not wholesome. But there is an ability to hold to the essence of the person without condemning them for their problems. We may think that if we met someone whom we knew had done some atrocious deeds, such as Saddam Hussein, we could not have compassion. But this is exactly where compassion is such a powerful way of viewing someone. With compassion, it is possible to see the man for what he is—a suffering, deluded human being worthy of compassion, despite having done what he did. There is no contradiction unless we fall into the view that the person and their actions are the same. If we can separate these out, then we may still condemn his actions and have compassion for the suffering nature that must have given rise to them.

Compassion does not grow from ideals of perfection, but from the recognition and acceptance of our human fallibility. The basis of compassion is a deep, empathic resonance with how vulnerable, fallible, and imperfect we are as humans, despite our efforts. If we can allow fallibility in ourselves without judging ourselves for it, we can begin to do so with others.

I have seen clients in therapy who have no capacity to accept their failings. They demand of themselves that they be perfect, infallible, and right. This is usually accompanied by a rigorous, harsh, judgmental side, which constantly berates them for not being good enough. There is no compassion in this inner reality, making it very hard for them to have compassion for others. When I was younger, I also had a very harsh internal critic and found it extremely difficult to allow myself to get things wrong and be fallible. It has only been through increasingly accepting myself as I am that I have found the capacity to be compassionate towards others.

Compassion is a quality of holding—a holding environment that can support others and care without becoming invasive or controlling of another's vulnerability. This is also a holding that is not afraid of the pain someone may be going through. As a therapist, I can affirm that both of these aspects have always felt crucial to the therapeutic context, but they are equally important in any situation where we are caring for another. Invasion of another implies that we might want to take charge of and sort out someone's suffering state in a way that is inappropriate. What clients need in therapy is someone holding, not rescuing or trying to make his or her problems better. There is a delicate balance involved in being able to remain present and in touch with a person's distress without trying to turn it into something else because we cannot bear it.

Compassionate holding requires an ability to stay with something a person is going through and to not panic because it is so painful. How much can we bear another's pain without interfering with it and without becoming overemotionally involved? If someone is in a place of depression, how comfortable are we with that, or do we try to do something to make it different? When I have been in periods of depression myself, what I have almost always needed has been someone simply able to stay present and to be understanding, not someone who will suggest that I snap out of it, or who tries to be positive.

Again, this is not to imply we should do nothing. Compassion can become active when the circumstances necessitate it. But taking someone's pain or problems away is not always the most wise or skillful thing to do. Compassion requires the wisdom to know what is useful. There are many times when people learn and grow from their distress or pain. To simply take it away is not necessarily the best answer. If someone comes to us with depression and the first thing we do is to provide an antidepressant, we could be preventing this person from going through a process that is deeply transformational. For many people, depression naturally unfolds when given the right supportive conditions. If we simply anesthetize the pain, we do not usually heal the root causes.[52]

Sometimes we may feel we are powerless to help or make things different. At such times, we have to learn to be with our own feelings of powerlessness or hopelessness. I can sometimes feel this in the therapeutic context when someone seems painfully stuck. I begin to pick up the sense of powerlessness or despair a client may feel, which cannot easily be overcome by finding a quick solution or strategy. When I feel this, often the most beneficial thing I can do is to simply name the sense of despair and hopelessness that is present as compassionately as I am able, allowing it to be what it is without trying to make it different.

We may feel a similar sense of powerlessness or hopelessness when we see some of the atrocities going on in the world and know there is so little we can personally do. Compassion can sometimes make us feel so sensitive it can be unbearable in the face of so much suffering. We may feel it is all too much or that we are hopeless to make things any different. It is at these moments that we may need to place ourselves in relation to the presence of universal compassion, however we choose to describe it. I have often felt that the only way to cope with the enormity of what I see around me is by offering it up, so to speak, by placing it in the greater hold of some transpersonal element of my spiritual life. This can take different forms in different traditions, but in Buddhism, it is where we seek "refuge" in the Buddhas as the embodiment of enlightened compassion. In the Tibetan tradition, the deity Chenrezig is seen as the embodiment of the compassionate quality of all the Buddhas. One way that we can then address this sense of being overwhelmed is to open to and be held by the compassionate presence of Chenrezig. We are inevitably limited in our capacity to bear great pain and distress in others, and in realizing this, we often need to surrender the ego to the greater resource of our buddha potential. In my own practice, when I do this in relation to the deity Chenrezig, I feel I am held by the presence of a power far greater than myself.

In the Tibetan paintings of what is known as "the wheel of life," the six realms of existence are depicted. These include the realms of the devas or gods, the jealous gods or Titans, humans, animals, wandering spirits, and hell-beings. If you look closely at the paintings, you will see depicted a monk often carrying some symbolic object. This figure is Chenrezig, the Buddha of compassion. He is depicted in each realm demonstrating that through the compassion of the Buddhas, there is a way to be released from suffering. He refers to the sense that with the presence of those beings, either Buddhas or bodhisattvas, who have the capacity to transcend this suffering world, there is hope. In the absence of awakened beings to show us a way out of the suffering of existence, things could indeed seem hopeless.

When, in light of others' suffering, we do become overwhelmed, it can lead to an emotionally paralyzed place. When this happens it is probably because we have become too immersed in the experience and lost some sense of our separation or objectivity. Lama

Yeshe once said, "Compassion is not sentimentality," in that it is not so much an emotional place, it is a feeling place. What I mean by this is that compassion requires a level of awareness that can remain objective and, to some degree, separate. This separateness is opposed to becoming lost in or drowning in the experience of suffering we see around us.

This is not an easy place to inhabit, but is necessary if we are to be of benefit to others. If we become too emotionally involved, we lose the capacity to see things clearly. I can see this in my work; if I was to become too drawn into a client's pain and distress, I would not be able to help. Conversely, there are those people who, in the face of someone's pain, cannot remain in contact with what is going on, and disconnect. This disconnection means there is no sense of someone being present with their distress. To hold a place of compassion with another's pain, it is necessary to remain present and aware. Compassionate presence is one of the most valuable and healing qualities we can offer another person when we are with them in times of suffering. This can be important for a relationship to individuals; it is not always so easy in relationship to the enormity of collective suffering.

What begins to be apparent from the practice of compassion is that we need to have a level of emotional and psychological maturity to truly embody the quality of compassion. Perhaps we can see that this is why the practice of compassion is some way down the road in this evolution of the development of bodhichitta. We need to have certain psychological preparation before compassion can be fully embodied. We need to have a relatively healthy, stable sense of identity that has dealt with some of its emotional wounding and has uncovered aspects of the shadow. Once there is a degree of psychological robustness, then the impact of others' suffering can enable the expression of compassion rather than emotional overwhelm or psychological disintegration. For many of us, when we are confronted with powerful and overwhelming suffering, it is too much to survive, and so we close down to it. One could see this as a necessary response to trauma to enable us to survive. We have to shut down. This is how some who return from war zones or famine manage to cope with the trauma they have witnessed. They have needed to protect themselves from the depth of pain they see. This is nevertheless not a healthy place to remain, shut down and cut off from feeling. At some point, the trauma must be addressed if it is not to impair emotional and psychological health.

This is partly why the bodhisattva is called "the awakening warrior," because he or she develops the strength to maintain a relationship to suffering in the world and remain compassionate, whole, and present. This strength is cultivated gradually: it is learned through experience and a growing capacity to bear others' pain and suffering, retain a sense of awareness, and maintain the capacity to remain in relation to it. We must understand our own limitations and develop compassion gradually.

Compassion can have a quality of gentle care, but it can also express something more robust and even tough. I have seen the tough side of compassion expressed by lamas who reprimand their monks. When parents hold their children with compassion, this tougher aspect of an expression of boundaries is vital. When I am with my own children, I often need to show firm limits to prevent them from acting in ways that would be harmful to themselves and others. Compassion in this respect is the protector that creates a safe environment for what is vulnerable.

It is for this reason that one of the most important deities practiced within the Tibetan tradition, Chenrezig, the Buddha of compassion, is associated with the dharma protector known as Mahakala. Mahakala is understood to be the wrathful aspect of Chenrezig and, as such, is seen as the wrathful face of compassion. It is this face that is needed in certain circumstances when there is the potential violation of someone's vulnerability. In this respect, compassion is not something that is meek and ineffective. It has a capacity to be firm, strong, and even fierce when necessary.

As we begin to explore the cultivation of compassion in our meditations, we can slowly discover some of the qualities I have mentioned here. Our capacity to feel compassion must begin with ourselves and those immediately close to us. As this grows, we can then start to expand the scope of our compassion to embrace a larger dimension of collective suffering as we recognize it around the world. In my own practice, I have found that some of the qualities I have described come more naturally than others. Particularly through my work as a psychotherapist, I have found a growing sense of my capacity to stay present with an individual's pain. What I still sometimes find overwhelming, however, is the immensity of suffering I see in places around the world that experience extreme catastrophe. Equally, there are certain experiences I see, such as severe suffering in children, which cause me to disconnect. What has become very clear to me, however, is that as my heart opens and my fear diminishes, my capacity to remain in touch with my feelings grows and my sense of compassion deepens and expands.

Loving-kindness

Within the verses of the "four immeasurable thoughts," which comprise a series of virtues (loving-kindness, compassion, sympathetic joy, equanimity) and Buddhist meditation practices designed to cultivate those virtues, is the phrase "how wonderful it would be if all beings were endowed with happiness and the causes of happiness."[53] Within the Buddhist world, this could be seen as the essence of loving-kindness. The expression of openness and care that comes with love brings with it a sense of connectedness and relationship that holds another dear and wishes to move towards him or her. This quality of heart opening is opposed to the tendency many of us have to remain distant, aloof, and closed. Loving-kindness wants to respond and engage and not remain distant.

Love is something we give off; it is more of an outward movement and expression of warmth and care, like the radiance of the sun. This warmth can be something that is felt as a general presence in the atmosphere, and it can equally be more focused and directed. It is expressed in how we act and in how we respond as "love made visible." We see this love in the care and concern we put into what we do. I have often sensed when I visit a particular cathedral close to where I used to live that the craftsmen put a huge amount of love into their work. They put their hearts into it.

The connection of love with the heart brings with it the pain of seeing the suffering of those we love. This is a very powerful experience for parents. Our love can open us to the experience of children, making it hard to bear the times when they are struggling or suffering. It is about being able to watch our child go off into the world and knowing that there's no way we should hold them back. Of course, love and attachment are sometimes closely connected, but it would be too simplistic to say that the pain we feel in relation to the suffering of one we love is because of our attachment. When we love, we open to the other and become more intimately in touch with the desire for them to be happy and the pain of seeing that they are not.

Love is outward moving and carries with it a sense of generosity of heart that is willing to give and share our love. Love radiates a quality that can touch the heart of those who can receive it and enable an opening and sense of connectedness. Often, when clients have spoken of the lack of love they experienced in their childhood, they gave the sense of a thirst or hunger that has never been satiated. Love is like a drink for those who are dry and thirsty; it is a nourishing food for those who have been starved. Love can fill and satisfy us, enabling us to feel we are enough.

Love can be profoundly ecstatic, and I do not mean the sexual love associated with tantra. This ecstatic quality of love is a kind of absorption that may be in relationship to an individual but may exist equally as a sense of the divine. This love can envelop us and melt our sense of ego contraction, opening us to something beyond individual limitation or boundaries. This is the immeasurable quality of love that is considered in the four Brahmavihāras or "four immeasurable thoughts." Love is a sense of unified oneness with life and others that brings warmth and nourishment. This love may be a kind of surrender to a sense of the divine—what the Greeks called *agape*, a sublime surrender.

For some, this quality of love is found through devotional faith in the divine, the Hindu sense of *bhakti*. For others, this quality of experience can seem totally alien. I often hear clients say that they yearn for some presence of divine love and yet find it inaccessible.

Does love in this sense come from without or within? From a Buddhist point of view, it is something that we can open to in ourselves and that, in doing so, we may well experience as something transpersonal and beyond our ego limitations. To awaken and embody this quality can have profound consequences in relation to those around us.

My own teacher Lama Thubten Yeshe was someone whose capacity to radiate a sense of love seemed immeasurable. He would sign his letters "Big Love Lama," and that was exactly what he had—big love. Having been a recipient of his love, I could see how much those around him were thirsty for what he offered. While I lived in India, I became very aware of how much Lama Yeshe's students, my peers and I, were hungry for contact with him. There were times when seeing this hunger in myself and those around me made me feel somewhat repelled by the urgency to have contact. When I saw this in myself I tended to withdraw, feeling somewhat ashamed, rather than be caught in the clamor. It would feel like being caught in a feeding frenzy.

Perhaps we in the West are particularly thirsty for love, so that when it is offered it is hard for us to know how to be with it. When we meet those who have a capacity for a powerful expression of love, we may find that we respond in different ways. For some, it may bring out a desperate need that makes them grasp at the source. For others, the presence of what is so sorely needed is almost too unbearable to receive. Can we receive love when it is given? Can we trust it? Do we feel able to open to what it offers and go beyond our fears?

Sometimes those who express their love can do so in a way that is too bright, too overwhelming, lacking a sense of containment. For others, love becomes an expression of a deep yearning to merge and lose a sense of separate self. Both of these reflect a loss of boundary. Love is not about losing the capacity to retain a sense of self, leading to a kind of unconscious, infantile regression. Some may yearn for this merged state with the mother,[54] mistaking it for the boundlessness of awakening, but this state would be both unconscious and psychologically detrimental to the individuation process.

As Longchenpa implied in his teachings on the four Brahmavihāras or "four immeasurables," when love becomes too caught up in this unconscious attachment, we have lost the objectivity that holds a sense of separate self. It is in this circumstance that we need to come back to compassion as the means to create objectivity and separation. Awareness and compassion help us come out of the regressive, merged state.

A female colleague I have discussed this with also found that the expression of love she gives towards some of her male clients was desperately needed but could easily become confused with their sexuality. One of the reasons those who have been abused in childhood often struggle with love in relationship to parental figures is that this is often mixed with sexuality. For example, disciples of teachers who need the love of the teacher can often mistakenly see sexuality as part of this relationship.

Clearly, sexuality can be part of an expression of love in our relationships. It can also be something mistakenly sought after as a means of feeling loved. I have known women who describe how they went through a phase of sexual promiscuity because they were desperate for love and confused the two. I have equally known men who confuse their need for sexual satisfaction with a need for love. How often I have heard women say that they wanted a loving intimacy, and the man wanted sex.

Just as with compassion, there can be a tougher side to love, which is not all sweetness and light. It can also be about tearing and rending. I have often felt the times that I have been really tested by my teachers as an expression of their love. I have always felt very aware of my teacher Lama Yeshe's love for me. But from that place of love, he would sometimes put me through things that were unbelievably painful because he was creating the conditions for me to change and grow. This may have required that on some level I needed to be taken to pieces. It was in these circumstances that I had to trust in his wisdom to know what was of benefit to me. When we are speaking of "tough love," the wisdom to know the consequences or effects is very important so that we are not simply being wounded or wounding someone.

In love there can also be pain, a pain that is part of a healing process. We sometimes do not change without pain. Just as the intensity of suffering in the world around us can feel overwhelming, so too it can be hard to bear the intensity of pain felt when someone we love suffers. The Greeks called this *pathos*. When I see my sons suffer in their lives it can be excruciating to witness, especially when there is sometimes nothing I can do about it. I cannot just take their pain away, even though I may wish to. In this love it can feel as though my heart is being torn.

I have not personally found the cultivation of love as easy as that of compassion because I have found the potential pain associated with love to be something hard to bear. I have known I could open and feel love but sometimes felt the consequence would be too great. Fear, I have felt, closes the heart and when the heart opens to love, it does so unreservedly. This openness leaves us with the immediacy of a connection that is deeply moving but also can be frighteningly vulnerable.

This has had implications for me as a man as well as a therapist. I have found that love is not always something men easily express or acknowledge. To show love is to show a softening that the world of men has not historically been comfortable with. Often, as the gateway of love opens, so our unmet needs emerge. As a therapist, my experience of love has touched on the potential taboo that loving someone could lead to a loss of boundaries. It has been liberating to come to the place where it is possible to genuinely love clients and express that love without any sense that I needed something in return. Having clear boundaries and a sense of my own capacity to be relatively contained and separate has been important in this, especially with female clients. Even so, to know it is possible to deeply love and still retain a clear sense of boundary has been an invaluable discovery in my work.

Variations of Tonglen

Over time, many variations of tonglen have emerged as it is applied in practice. This gives validity to the idea that this practice can be creatively designed to suit the individual. As I said earlier, I have known Christians using a variation of tonglen that includes a visualization of Christ.

When I first encountered this practice, it was taught by a number of traditional Tibetan teachers who used a particular visualization. I was asked to imagine being seated on a high place such as a hill surrounded by countless sentient beings. I was then directed to reflect upon the sufferings of those around and living within the different realms of existence, including the human and animal realms, the hell realms, wandering spirit realms, and so on. Having reflected upon their suffering, I was instructed to consider the wish to take on their suffering as visualized in the form of smoke or blackness drawn in with each breath. I was taught to visualize the "self-cherishing" mind located at the heart in the form of a black lump. As I breathed in the smoky suffering, it would be cast against this black lump of self-cherishing with the intention of totally destroying it.

Once I had spent some time with this visualization, the intention would change, and with the thought of benefiting those around by giving happiness, I was taught to breathe out radiant light. This light emerged from the heart and was then exhaled through the nostrils as a light of loving-kindness that went out to all those around, bringing happiness, joy, and release from suffering.

Working with this particular visualization has often not felt particularly comfortable. There seemed to be something too aggressive in the "attack" on my heart that would feel quite painful. It was only later, when I shifted to a more gentle visualization that dissolved the heart rather than striking it, that this pain went. I began to feel that perhaps I needed to be more compassionate towards my own lack of openness in the heart rather than attack it as though it was bad.

On another occasion, I was taught a version of this practice in which one would first visualize a deity such as Chenrezig seated upon one's head or in the heart. This was to enable the sense that through the blessings of Chenrezig, one would be able to take on suffering. Chenrezig acted as a kind of catalyst and support to transform the suffering into light.

A variation of this practice that I have also been given is to visualize oneself either as the deity Chenrezig or Tara, and then perform the breath process. This time, rather than visualizing the black lump at the heart, I would visualize that as the dark suffering is breathed in, it is transformed into a light energy as soon as it touches the heart, where one envisions a seed syllable.[55] This light is then breathed out as loving-kindness. In one practice I have seen described, a diamond within a lotus is visualized at the heart.[56] Whether visualizing a seed syllable or diamond, one should imagine that this transforms the incoming dark cloud of suffering into a light of loving-kindness that is radiated out in the next breath.

In the practice of tonglen, it is often suggested that we should first become familiar with taking on and accepting our own suffering. This can be done simply by considering our own emotional or physical problems and then willingly accepting them as they are as we breathe in, rather than struggling against them and fighting ourselves. To make this more effective, it can be very helpful to visualize yourself in front of you and then spend time connecting to particular difficulties you might have. When working with clients in a mentoring setting who have suffered significant trauma or difficulties in childhood that are still emotionally disturbing, I have often suggested that people visualize themselves as that child in front of them. The person then spends time feeling into the nature of the childhood difficulties and eventually begins a process of tonglen. Meditating in this way has helped them to begin to love themselves with their wounding and pain rather than reject the child within because it is unacceptable.

On one occasion, I was speaking with a woman who had begun to recognize that she had a deep-rooted loathing towards herself as a child. This was accompanied by a sense of shame and repulsion for how she felt she was as a child. The effect of this inner conflict was to shut off any real emotional connection to herself because she felt so deeply unacceptable as a child. She blamed her inner child for all the problems she had in her life, with the effect that she was continually abandoning herself emotionally and yet tending to consider that others were abandoning her because she was so "bad." As this patterning became more obvious, I suggested she might use the tonglen practice by visualizing herself as a little girl coming into the space before her and then beginning to open up a relationship. At first, she felt huge resistance and then, as she began to actually see the suffering of this child before her and the unfortunate circumstances of her life, she started to take on and accept her suffering. In time, she was even able to begin to give out a sense of kindness and love that wished her to be happy. Gradually, a healing took place that went some way towards repairing a deep inner split.

When practicing tonglen in relation to others, it can be helpful to begin by recalling images that give rise to particularly strong feelings of compassion and loving-kindness. This may involve those you are close to, such as children or loved ones, for whom the more natural response is to feel compassion. As this experience grows, it becomes more possible to use the tonglen process in relation to those with whom we have some difficulty. It can then be very beneficial to visualize someone who troubles us or who has caused us some sort of harm and then go through the process of tonglen. Visualize taking on the suffering that arises from their problems and confusion, and then sending out a light of loving-kindness. As we spend time with this process in meditation, it can change our view and reaction to someone in a very beneficial way.

Another variety of practice is to reflect on problems or illnesses we experience currently and then recall all those whose suffering is probably equal or much worse. This may be very powerful if we are the kind of person who becomes depressed or downhearted when there are problems in our life. It helps us to realize that we are not the only one who is suffering in this way. It can aid us in letting go of the disposition to be caught in a self-preoccupied state. For example, if I have the flu or some similar ailment, I find it very useful to take on the suffering of all those who may be suffering in a similar way. On those occasions when I find myself laid out with illness, it is the one thing I can do that opens up my mind and my heart. I recently went through a period of terrible pain from an abcessed tooth and found that the tonglen practice was a great resource to diminish the disposition to close into a contracted space of pain and misery. It did not take the pain away, but it certainly changed my attitude towards it. Whatever the hardship is in our life, if we include it in our meditation, we can think of those around who are suffering just as much, if not worse. Our relationship to hardship and pain changes as we let go. It can feel less distressing and overwhelming. Our mind begins to open up and feel more spacious, and our heart can begin to feel a greater concern and compassion for those who suffer similarly.

As our practice grows and deepens, we will become increasingly able to expand our field of vision to encompass many different contexts we are aware of throughout the world. We can then draw on things we have some particular contact with or see in the news. There are so many examples of suffering in the world that offer us the chance to practice and open our hearts.

The visualization I explain in the following meditation is a form that I have found very powerful personally and which incorporates some of the above features.

Meditation 4: Tonglen meditation

Begin by bringing your attention back to the natural rising and falling of the breath. Allow time for your awareness to settle.

Then imagine that you are seated on a small hill so that you are able to see a long distance. Begin to visualize before and around you those that you are close to in your life, those that you live with and work amongst, including those you do not have a good relationship with. Gradually expand the scope of your awareness to include those who live farther away and who inhabit the planet with you. This can also include the animals and creatures that live around you.

Spend time reflecting upon the lives of those that are closer to you. Include in this category people who may be troublesome to you. Consider the struggles and difficulties that these people have and the kind of suffering they all experience: sufferings of sickness, of unhappiness, stress, emotional problems, and so on.

Then consider the thought: "How wonderful it would be if all of these people were free from suffering and the causes of suffering.

May they be free from suffering and its cause. May I free them from suffering and its cause. Bless me to be able to do this."

Visualize that as you take your in-breaths, you begin to draw all of their suffering out of those before you in the form of grey smoke. Breathe this into you and imagine that at your heart it begins to be transformed into a light of compassion and love, opening your heart. Spend time with this visualization, considering that this is really releasing those before you from their suffering.

After some minutes, consider the thought: "How wonderful it would be if all of these people were endowed with happiness and its cause. May they be endowed in this way. May I endow them in this way. Please bless me to be able to do this."

Following this thought, begin to visualize that with the out-breath you breathe out a light of loving-kindness that emerges from your heart and goes out to those around you, filling their hearts and minds with a quality of happiness and ease. Spend some time with this visualization, considering that they are truly endowed with a greater sense of peace and happiness in their lives.

After some time, begin to bring these two visualizations together so that with each in-breath you breathe in the suffering of those around, and with each out-breath you breathe out a light of loving-kindness.

After some time, stop this process and simply remain with what you are feeling.

TONGLEN MEDITATION ON WORLD SUFFERING
This is an optional continuation of the previous practice.

Return to the visualization of those before and around you.

This time, begin to explore the lives of those around you in a broader sense. Consider those places in the world where there are severe hardships and trouble. This may be in the form of war, famine, social upheaval, and other hardship. It is useful to consider those places around the world where there is currently trouble, where your awareness is fresh. Spend time deepening your awareness of specific places and of people's suffering. Try to allow a sense of the pain of this.

Then return to the thought: "How wonderful it would be if all of these people were free from suffering and the causes of suffering. May they be free from suffering and its cause. May I free them from suffering and its cause. Bless me to be able to do this."

Then visualize that as you take your in-breath you begin to draw all of the suffering out of those in these places in the form of grey smoke. Breathe this into you and imagine that at your heart it begins to be transformed into a light of compassion and love, opening your heart. Spend time with this visualization, considering that this is really releasing them from their suffering.

After some minutes, consider the thought: "How wonderful it would be if all of these people were endowed with happiness and its cause. May they be endowed in this way. May I endow them in this way. Please bless me to be able to do this."

Following this thought, begin to visualize that with the out-breath you breathe out a light of loving-kindness that goes out to those you visualize, clearing the painful conditions in which they live and filling their bodies, hearts, and minds with a quality of happiness and ease. Spend some time with this visualization, considering that they are truly endowed with a greater sense of peace and happiness in their lives.

Finally, begin to bring these two visualizations together so that with each in-breath you breathe in the suffering of those around, and with each out-breath you breathe out a light of loving-kindness.

After some time, stop this process and simply remain with what you are feeling.

Close the meditation with the dedication: Through this meditation practice may I be able to awaken to my full potential in order to bring benefit to every living being without exception, to enable them to also awaken to their full potential.

* * *

An alternative version of this practice is to begin with a visualization of yourself before you. You can then spend time reflecting upon the sufferings of your life and particularly your childhood or your inner emotional problems. Then with the same attitude, begin to breathe in this suffering and breathe out the light of loving-kindness. This approach can be a powerful way of beginning to change our inner relationship to ourselves if there tend to be particularly negative or self-destructive feelings.

CHAPTER ELEVEN

The Supreme Wish

WITHIN BUDDHIST CIRCLES, the idea of will is sometimes seen as problematic. How do we live with a sense of will that is not merely based in the ego's need to assert itself in the world? How do we recognize the need to have a quality of intention in our life, or indeed, our spiritual life, without it being dominated by the ego's aggressive desire to get what it wants? How, we might ask, is the will relevant in the context of bodhichitta, where there is an expressed intention to become a buddha for the welfare of others?

Our contemplation of the qualities of love and compassion practiced within the meditation of tonglen lead naturally to what is called the "supreme wish" or sometimes the "great will." An evolution in the nature of our will may begin with a wish that leads to a positive aspiration, which gradually progresses to a significant engagement of will. In the verses of the "four immeasurable thoughts" mentioned earlier, this shift is apparent if we look more closely:

> How wonderful it would be if all beings were free of
> suffering and the causes of suffering
> May they be free of suffering and its causes
> May I free them in this way
> Please bless me guru Buddhas to be able to do this.

The verses begin "How wonderful it would be"—with a kind of wishful desire for something to arise that would benefit others. This wish progresses to a more aspirational thought—"May they be free of suffering and its causes"—as the quality of intention begins to shift. This leads to a genuine desire to act—an act of will—expressed in the line "May I free them in this way," which is often translated simply as "I will free them in this way." This may be seen as the ego's intention to act, but what begins to unfold is a process that must shift to a deeper level, beyond the ego's will. This shift is partly suggested by the plea, "Please bless me guru Buddhas to be able to do this."

In the journey of individuation, we will come to a place where it is necessary that we let go of the ego's will and yield to a greater or deeper intention. In the language of Jung, this is where the ego lets go of the assumption that it is the primary determining factor in the journey and gives way to the intention of the Self. Jung recognized that this shift is crucial in the individuation process because the ego is limited in its insight into the potential unfolding of the journey. We need to open to and trust in a deeper center of wisdom that can guide us.

This change can be very challenging. It is often brought about by the recognition that the way we have been directing our life has become narrow, self-limiting, and egotistical. We may become acutely aware that our ego intention cannot make the things we desire happen. We may begin to see that so long as our egotistical ambitions color our aims and goals, even within our spiritual journey there will always be an emotional undertone that exposes our attachment to the outcome. There is a certain irony in the ego striving to attain buddhahood when, as Chögyam Trungpa once said, the ego will never see itself crowned king.

Letting go of ego intention and opening to a greater, deeper intention is an act of surrender that can be unsettling. We may not have the same sense of control or the same secure sense that we know where we are going. The ego until this point has needed to be in control and dominant in its grasp on life. Now it is being asked to surrender this dominant position and allow something to unfold from a deeper place. The ego moves from what has been safe and familiar patterning to something unfamiliar and potentially even more powerful.

I have seen this process take place in many of my clients and have also felt it in my own life. There can often be a sense of what was familiar breaking down to enable a new process to unfold. I have felt the uncertainty and lack of solidity this process can bring at various times of my life. What was an old, well-established mode of living is suddenly thrown into question and I have to let go and open to what may emerge. At these times, it is easy to potentially go into an anxious, controlling state out of a need to gain certainty and security. If instead I can remain open and allow a deeper sense of what is developing to take me where I need to go, this anxiety can fade. It requires a surrender that Ian Gordon Brown, my transpersonal psychotherapy teacher, once described as the shift from "I will" to "Thy will be done."

We may see this as the time when we open to the divine, the transpersonal, the Self, our buddha potential, or however we choose to label it. There will certainly be a sense that this is bigger than the little "me," the ego-me. We may also have a sense that we are being asked to engage in something with an uncertain outcome but which requires that we trust in the process.

For the cultivation of bodhichitta, this is a significant moment. Rather than acting from the ego as the center of intention, we shift to a deeper undercurrent of intention that will flow through our life like a powerful river carrying us along. Once we are willing to let go into this stream of intention, its momentum can propel us forward. This is expressed in the part of the bodhisattva prayer from the *Heruka Tantra* that says, "In order to liberate sentient beings, I offer myself immediately to all the Buddhas."[57]

Once we begin to align ourselves with this greater will or archetypal intent, to use Jung's term, we will often feel that we are doing what is true for us. We may have a sense of meaning in our life that has taken on a different proportion. This meaning has less to do with what we are doing practically; rather, it is the undercurrent that motivates what we are doing. In this respect, the task is somehow less crucial.

In talking to clients it is often important to make the distinction between the task they may wish to find to make their life meaningful, and the underlying quality of intention that runs through their life. Once this distinction is made, it becomes possible to allow the task to emerge because they have aligned themselves with a quality of intention that carries the focus of meaning. This may go against the increasingly popular idea in the conventional world of setting one's goals or establishing "vision statements." The world that needs these more solidly formed ideas of a goal is very much the world of the ego. The ego needs form to feel safe and in control. With the shift of will I am speaking of here, however, there is a sense in which we have to relinquish that need for clear forms.

In my own journey, I have found this shift important because it places less emphasis on the specific task and more on the feeling of trust in what is unfolding. As a Buddhist, this has meant that when I do place my root of intention in the hands of the Buddhas, so to speak, I feel I can let go and relax. This does not imply that I should do nothing. I can feel that my personal intention is still engaged but is aligned with a deep knowing. There is an expression, "Trust in God but tether your camel."

The result of this alignment with a deeper intention is that I can feel I am being true to myself and can really give myself to what I am doing wholeheartedly, without the sense of limitation that comes from fear. It also requires that I listen deeply to what I feel I am moved to engage with.

When we surrender and engage our intention in this way, it becomes the Great Will or Supreme Wish that runs through whatever we do in life. At first, this may seem somewhat self-conscious, but gradually it can become like the river that has run underground. As Shantideva says, it flows on even in our sleep.

Meditation 5: Cultivating the willingness to surrender

Begin by bringing your attention back to the natural rising and falling of the breath.

After some minutes, visualize that you are seated on a hill with a distant view. Begin to imagine around you those you are close to, those you work with and live amongst, and those you find difficult and who are problematic to you. Open this out to all those who inhabit the planet with you, including all of the creatures on the planet and the planet itself.

Begin to remind yourself of the fortune of your own life, the qualities and endowments of your life—your freedom to practice the dharma. Recall the fragility of this life—that death is definite but that you have no way of knowing when it will happen. Then reflect on the extraordinary value of your life: to be able to awaken to the full potential of your buddha nature, not only for your own benefit, but for the welfare of all those you see around you.

Following this, spend a while visualizing Buddha Shakyamuni seated upon a lotus sun and moon seat in the sky above these people surrounded by an assembly of other Buddhas and deities. Then consider from your heart the thought: "In order to benefit all these beings who are living with so much suffering and confusion and through whose kindness I live, I offer myself immediately to all the Buddhas."

With this thought in mind, try to visualize all the different aspects of yourself, your life, your work, your possessions, and your relationships being offered up to the Buddhas like a mandala offering. Then offer the prayer from your heart: "Whatever is beneficial for me to serve the welfare of others through the skills and qualities that I have, may I receive the blessings of the Buddhas to make possible."

Remain with the feeling left by this prayer for some time. Then visualize that the Buddhas absorb into Shakyamuni Buddha, who then comes to your head and melts into golden light, which dissolves into your body, blessing you.

CHAPTER TWELVE

The Awakening Mind

IN THE MAHAYANA TRADITION, motivation is considered to be of great importance. We are asked to consider that the actions of our life are made with the motivation of bodhichitta. My early years with my Tibetan teachers were marked by a constant reminder that it is necessary to cultivate the "correct motivation" before I engage in any practice.

Many things may motivate us in our life and even in our practice of Buddhism, but from a Mahayana Buddhist point of view, the most profound motivation is considered to be the intention to attain the state of a buddha for the welfare of others. This begs the question, however, of whether we understand the notion of buddhahood itself or, indeed, whether we can ever actually understand the state of a buddha from our relatively limited human position. I have spent many years studying this from a somewhat intellectual perspective but still find it extremely hard, if not impossible, to actually conceive of what a buddha experiences. I can relate to buddhahood from a more intuitive sense, as a vision of wholeness depicted in the wonderful images of Buddhas that I find so inspiring as a painter of Tibetan Buddhist icons (*tangkhas*). I have had clues from the encounters I have had with some particularly highly gifted and realized Tibetan lamas such as the Dalai Lama. However, I am still left somewhat in the dark. How can I know if the Dalai Lama is Buddha or not? It is a little like looking at two ships on the ocean horizon and wondering if they are the same distance away. It is extremely difficult to tell.

Whether we hold the notion of buddhahood to be a state of wholeness, completion, or perfection, it remains something that still lies beyond our ordinary comprehension. This does not make it unreachable, but from our human perspective, it is nevertheless hard to imagine. If bodhichitta is to be tied specifically to the notion of complete awakening or buddhahood as a goal, then this has to be on the basis of great faith, or we need some other way to make a connection. We may naturally find great inspiration from a vision of wholeness. This was certainly my experience when I first began to encounter images of the Buddha and the various deity forms depicted in tangkhas. I found that as visions of wholeness, these images touched me more deeply than intellectual knowledge because they reached a place of deep, archetypal knowing rooted in the unconscious. It is a kind of intuitive knowing that our essential nature is pristine, whole, divine, or whatever terms we choose to use.

Jung recognized the significance and power of archetypal images of wholeness, as they hold a kind of numinosity for us.[58] I have seen this in my own life when as a young man I encountered images from the East that touched me deeply even though at the time, I did not really know what I was seeing.[59] When we encounter such images, Jung would say that it brings us into relationship with the underlying archetypal intent that these images hold. Jung recognized that this type of image or vision is a natural aspect of our psyche that may become active at certain times in our life and move us deeply towards wholeness, even if we are not totally conscious of the fact.

What this implies is that we each carry a natural "instinct" towards wholeness that may or may not be conscious. It is a quality that is reflected in images we encounter outside of us, but it must be understood as an inner potential. While Jung saw this as the Self, in Buddhism we see this as our intrinsic buddha potential, our buddha nature.

The *Uttaratantrashastra,* which Asanga received from Maitreya, speaks of our buddha nature as being like a golden statue wrapped in rags, a seed within the rotting fruit, honey within the swarm of bees.[60] These metaphors of our innate wholeness are like the "pebble dropped into the pool that touches the bottom without disturbing the surface."⁶¹ If we allow ourselves to be truly touched by them, they offer a profound confidence that we have the potential for health, wholeness, and peace within us.

What this means for me is that this vision of wholeness grows and changes, is fluid and a constant revelation as I grow and change. It is not a fixed frame that has been set in stone or, indeed, in time. It is like a form that is slowly being revealed from the mist of my own obscurity of mind. Our experience of wholeness is alive and forever somewhat mysterious.

On some level, I feel that I neither need nor wish to know totally where I am going. Do I need to know exactly what buddhahood is in order to generate bodhichitta, or could this knowledge become something too solid and therefore lacking in mystery? Might this then even become a kind of obstacle in my path?

Indications are that buddhahood is a process rather than a goal and that there is an endless unfolding so long as relative and ultimate realities are in a constant dance. The Buddha himself said that he could not perceive an end to samsara, the cycle of existence. If this implied he could not see an end to relative truth, relative forms, and appearances, then the task of an awakened one is to remain within this dance of truths manifesting enlightened activity as far as the ocean's horizon and beyond.

Meditation 6: Cultivating clear intention

Bring your attention back to the natural rising and falling of the breath.

After some minutes, feel into your body and sense where the quality of intention to act in your life emerges from. This may be your heart or navel. Tune into this place of intention and remain for a while.

Then visualize that some way off in the future is your awakened state of buddhahood. You may wish to visualize this in the form of a deity or the Buddha. Then from the seat of intention within, send out your intention towards that Buddha image. Make a deep inner connection of your intention aligned with your future buddhahood.

Stay for some minutes with that feeling so that it becomes deeply aligned, and watch what kind of feelings arise as you do so.

Visualize that between you at this moment in your life and that future buddhahood, a deep river is flowing on. Allow yourself to settle into that river of unfolding. Then think: in order to benefit all sentient beings I myself will awaken this innate buddha potential.

Finish with a dedication: May I awaken to my full buddha potential in order to benefit all sentient beings to enable them to also awaken to their full potential.

CHAPTER THIRTEEN
The Paradox of Awakening

IN ATTEMPTING to explain some of the twists and turns on the journey towards the cultivation of bodhichitta, the awakening mind, I have tried to look at some of its psychological implications. As this quality of intention grows in our life, it is important to allow for the inevitability that our capacity to open and surrender, to love and serve deepens and strengthens as we uncover the aspects of ourselves that psychologically hinder the process. Learning from our errors and gaining a deeper relationship to our own psychological pathology is, in this respect, essential

What I have tried to include here are some of the ways in which our personal issues color our experience of the special meditation practices involved. The cultivation of bodhichitta then leads us to a paradox that is central to Buddhist understanding. It is said in many Tibetan teachings that bodhichitta can be understood on two levels. One is known as relative bodhichitta, while the other is called ultimate bodhichitta. We have explored at length the cultivation of relative bodhichitta as the intention to awaken for the benefit of sentient beings. Ultimate bodhichitta, however, is usually described as the realization of emptiness. Where these two meet is at a place of paradox.

We may develop a profound and powerful intention to awaken for the welfare of others and yet come to realize that the state of awakening is something that arises in the present. When we understand this paradox, we recognize that there is actually nowhere to go: no goal of the path other than to become fully present without obstruction.

As Buddhists, we are very familiar with speaking of a spiritual path and even delineating stages upon that path as we grow and develop our practice. With the growth of an intention such as the cultivation of bodhichitta, there is always the hazard of making where we are going more important than where we are. This is like the person who is so intent on practicing to gain enlightenment for the sake of others that he neglects the very people that he lives with. As I have mentioned, in my own journey I have seen this idealistic intention lead me to work very hard to attain a goal and sometimes cause me to become very narrow in my vision. When this happens, my capacity to be truly present goes, and I can barely recognize the fact because I am so focused on where I am going.

When we open to the meaning of ultimate bodhichitta, we move to a state of being that is not bound by the forms and creations of our relative mind. It is an opening to the underlying spacious and empty nature of reality. We shift from the reality of intentions to the place of pure being. In that state of awareness, we see the inseparability and interdependence of whatever arises. Therefore, there is no separate, substantial self to develop, and no evolutionary movement forward.

As I have written at length in *The Wisdom of Imperfection*, the bodhisattva has the qualities of a warrior that can be powerfully focused in overcoming obstacles in the path and taking up a challenge.[62] This willfulness, however, must be balanced with the recognition of when to stop and the capacity to surrender self-will. Unless we begin to include this understanding, our striving to attain the goal of enlightenment can become just another source of stress and confusion. As Chögyam Trungpa has written, "We go around and around, trying to improve ourselves through struggle, until we realize that the ambition to improve ourselves is itself the problem."[63]

So how do we bring together our understanding and experience of the growth of bodhichitta as a quality of intention with the need to let go and be present? Perhaps the answer is not so remarkable, as on some level it is something we must do with every aspect of our lives. Can we aim our intention in a certain direction and then let go, and not be attached to an outcome? If we can let go into the river of bodhichitta, then we can remain in the present and trust in its course because we have, to use a term in the *Heruka Tantra*, "offered ourselves to the Buddhas."[64]

The bodhisattva is sometimes compared to the peacock that can live on poisonous plants and transform them into the beautiful colors of its feathers.[65] It is certainly an attitude to life that engages with challenges rather than seeing life as a problem and running away or being a victim. The bodhisattva lives between worlds, between the rawness of our human fallibility as we face the challenges of our time and the vast, expansive peace of our innate clear light nature. He or she does not abandon one for the other, but remains in the tension of the two. Bringing these two dimensions of reality together does not bring comfort and ease, but it does generate a creative aliveness that is in touch with the suffering and the beauty of life in all its manifestations while recognizing it as the play of *dharmakaya*, of emptiness or nonduality. Resting in clear present awareness, the bodhisattva responds to the fleeting nature of appearances in a spontaneous, fresh, and creative way, as though riding a wave of reality as it comes into being. From this place, he or she can work in the world and be a vehicle for the wisdom, love, and compassion that is our buddha nature to manifest for the benefit of others.

CHAPTER FOURTEEN

Our Place in the World

I WOULD LIKE to end by approaching a subject that can be over-looked in our Buddhist life, and yet is an important aspect of a con-temporary understanding of bodhichitta. Within the Buddhist world in its original Eastern setting, there is a relationship to the forces of nature that is easily overlooked as Buddhism is transported to the West. For example, this relationship is present in the rituals of the tantric tradition in which offerings are made to local guardians and spirits to ask for support when doing practice. In Thailand, offer-ings are made to local spirits and guardians out of respect for their presence. When we look more deeply into this practice, we start to see that it is present because Buddhism developed in cultures that still see the natural world as sacred and filled with forces that we need to live alongside rather than disrespect. Meditators in the East respect the idea that the land holds forces that influence our lives in ways that are hidden yet significant. Meditation retreats and other rituals are not usually performed without first considering a rela-tionship to the environment within which they are performed, so as not to disturb the presence of elemental forces in the area. Seldom would buildings be constructed without first making offerings to the local spirits and guardians present in nature. However, in the West, we meditate in the sanitized environment of the local temple and seldom see the connection our practices have with nature.

While it may not be easy for many of us to take seriously the pres-ence of spirits and elemental forces in the environment, nevertheless it is beneficial to reconsider the sacred nature of the natural world.

It is a living presence that needs to be included in our expression of bodhichitta. When we consider the kindness of the mother, we should also consider the kindness of the earth in providing the very life that we need for nourishment. In most indigenous cultures, the earth *is* the great mother that sustains and provides for us even though we may continually abuse and defile its life. A Mexican Huichol teacher recently said to a group of Americans that if they could see the beauty of the earth as little as a couple of thousand years ago, they would die of grief seeing what has happened to it.

If we are to transform the adversity we encounter in our lives and in the larger global context, it will require a deeper relationship to the earth and perhaps a return to some understanding of the way indigenous cultures viewed this relationship. They felt great gratitude for the earth's gift of life and repaid that kindness with respect and harmony. They would not abuse this gift, for they believed this would destroy the relationship and lead to disaster, which, as we can begin to see, is actually happening. As Buddhist practitioners, we may begin to ask, how useful is our expression of bodhichitta if it does not also respond to the very source of life itself? Can we serve others and yet continue to overlook the presence of the planet that supports our life?

Bodhichitta is the opening of our heart to genuinely care and appreciate our life together on this earth without the fearful self-protection that is so much part of our materialistic culture. As such, bodhichitta can heal the alienation we so often feel with each other and also with the natural world. Once this undercurrent of meaning flows through our life, we will naturally begin to re-vision much of what has held significance to us. We will have a deep sense of our heart's calling in a way that can bring greater fulfillment, peace, and harmony. We will also have a greater recognition of our place in the world and our responsibility for what we can contribute both to others and to the natural world. When we open to the totality of life and recognize our interrelationship with all things, bodhichitta becomes an essential ingredient for a happy mind in the midst of possible stress, depression, anxiety, dissatisfaction, and insecurity.

Recently, I was sitting upon the granite remains of what was once a mountain we call in the U.K. a *tor*, looking out across a landscape that has been shaped through time into a wonderful natural sculpture. The beauty of the land with its heather- and gorse-covered hills, dipping into deep river valleys lined with ancient oaks and strewn with moss-covered rocks, always fills my heart with so much joy and peace. As I sat, I felt deeply the health of that land and its living presence and considered the lives of those who had for thousands of years inhabited the place, leaving their stone circles and bridges, shaping the dry stone walls, and grazing their sheep and cattle. The moorland feels ancient and yet is in constant flux as its moods and weather endlessly change. What I began to feel was a huge sense of love and gratitude, of humility and respect for the sacred presence of the land and the weather that supports our life. I had the sense that my life is so inextricably bound up with this land for my existence that I had to honor its beauty, its wildness, and its raw vitality. As I settled in that feeling I became aware that this echoed the same feeling I had had many years earlier when in Bodhgaya the lama Tara Tulku had momentarily given me a taste of his experience of bodhichitta. I realized that I cannot separate myself from the land and those billions of creatures that inhabit it; I can only, from the depth of my heart, try to care for its health so long as I am able. If I love this land and care for its well-being, why would I not wish to awaken for its welfare?

Dedication

MAY THOSE who benefit from this work awaken to their full potential and be of lasting value to every living being to enable them to also awaken to their full potential.

May we live with respect, harmony, love, and gratitude for the land that is the source of life, and may we be blessed with conditions favorable to the well-being of us all.

Notes

1 Individuation: "to denote a process of becoming a psychological 'individual,' that is, a separate, indivisible unity or whole." Jung, *The Archetypes and the Collective Unconscious*, p.275. "Individuation means becoming a single homogeneous being, and, insofar as 'in-dividuality' embraces our innermost, last and incomparable uniqueness, it also implies becoming one's own self. We could therefore translate 'individuation' as 'coming to selfhood' or 'self-realization.'" Jung, *Two Essays on Analytical Psychology*, p.171.

2 Shantideva, *A Guide to the Bodhisattva's Way of Life*, Chapter 1, verse 26.

3 Shantideva, *A Guide to the Bodhisattva's Way of Life*, Chapter 3, verse 31.

4 Shantideva, *A Guide to the Bodhisattva's Way of Life*, Chapter 3, verse 32.

5 Shantideva, *A Guide to the Bodhisattva's Way of Life*, Chapter 1, verse 5.

6 We can understand feelings in a number of ways that differentiate them from emotions. From one perspective, they form a relatively subtle sensitivity in response to a field of experience, whereas emotions are a more gross reactive expression. Often feelings are less conscious, whereas our emotions are outward and expressive—unless, of course, they are suppressed. Feelings do not have the ego-grasping charge of the emotions. For Jung, the "feeling function" is a way of knowing about and evaluating our experiences. It is a discriminating function— something feels right or feels wrong. In Tibetan Buddhism the term *tsorwa* refers to something which is a mix of feeling/sensation that is a response to contact with the environment.

7 This is a reference to Jung's four functions: thinking, feeling, intuition, and sensation.

8 Shantideva, *A Guide to the Bodhisattva's Way of Life*, Chapter 3, verses 29-32.

9 Preece, *The Wisdom of Imperfection*, Chapter 5.

10 This is a reference to an expression used in the sadhana of Chenrezig that he has narrow compassionate eyes like a loving parent for his only child.

11 Tarthang Tulku, *Openness Mind*.

12 Numinous: a term Jung borrowed from Rudolf Otto to describe a sense of awe and highly charged fascination.

13 Arya Maitreya and Asanga, *The Changeless Nature*, p. 34.

14 Stevens, *Archetype*, Chapter 9.

15 Shantideva, *A Guide to the Bodhisattva's Way of Life*, Chapter 4, verses 34-38.
16 Shantideva, *A Guide to the Bodhisattva's Way of Life*, Chapter 7, verses 47-48.
17 Shantideva, *A Guide to the Bodhisattva's Way of Life*, Chapter 1, verse 10.
18 Shantideva, *A Guide to the Bodhisattva's Way of Life*, Chapter 1, verse 12.
19 Shantideva, *A Guide to the Bodhisattva's Way of Life*, Chapter 3, verses 28-32.
20 Jung, *The Archetypes and the Collective Unconscious*, pp. 160 and 270; Jung, *Symbols of Transformation*, p. 510.
21 Jung, *Psychology and Alchemy*, fig. 25.
22 Shantideva, *A Guide to the Bodhisattva's Way of Life*, Chapter 1, verses 18-19.
23 Dalai Lama, *A Human Approach to World Peace, p. 7.*
24 Taken from a commentary by Geshe Rabten given in Dharamsala and transcribed for the FPMT.
25 Ibid.
26 Yeshe Tsondu, *The Essential Nectar of the Holy Doctrine*, verses 307-310, in Geshe Rabten, *The Essential Nectar*, pp. 225-226.
27 Shantideva, *A Guide to the Bodhisattva's Way of Life*, Chapter 6, verses 101 and 107.
28 Zopa Rinpoche, *The Wish-fulfilling Golden Sun*, p. 109.
29 Thogme Zangpo, *The Thirty-seven Practices of All Buddhas' Sons*, verse 5.
30 Jung, *Psychology and Alchemy*, p. 36; Anthony Stevens, *On Jung*, pp. 43-46.
31 Thogme Zangpo, *The Thirty-seven Practices of All Buddhas' Sons*, verse 17.
32 Shantideva, *A Guide to the Bodhisattva's Way of Life*, Chapter 6, verse 47.
33 Hillman, *Anima*.
34 Johnson, *He: Understanding Masculine Psychology*; Emma Jung, *Animus and Anima*.
35 Johnson, *We: Understanding the Psychology of Romantic Love*; *He: Understanding Masculine Psychology*; and *She: Understanding Feminine Psychology*. Hillman, *Anima*. Emma Jung, *Animus and Anima*.
36 Winnicott, *The Maturational Processes and the Facilitating Environment*, p. 75.
37 Yeshe Tsondu, *The Essential Nectar of the Holy Doctrine*, verses 314-317, in Geshe Rabten, *The Essential Nectar*, pp. 226-227.
38 Geshe Rabten teaching on bodhichitta
39 Winnicott, *The Maturational Processes and the Facilitating Environment*, pp. 57-58.
40 Jung, *The Archetypes and the Collective Unconscious*, p. 92.
41 Winnicott, *The Maturational Processes and the Facilitating Environment*, pp. 57-58.
42 Yeshe Tsondu, *The Essential Nectar of the Holy Doctrine*, verses 305 and 306, in Geshe Rabten, *The Essential Nectar*, p. 225.
43 Miller, *The Drama of Being a Child*, pp. 17-23.
44 Dharmarakshita, *The Wheel of Sharp Weapons*, verses 14-18.
45 Dharmarakshita, *The Wheel of Sharp Weapons*, verses 26-30.
46 Dharmarakshita, *The Wheel of Sharp Weapons*, verse 53.
47 E.g., this usage occurs in Tarthang Tulku's *Openness Mind*.
48 Preece, *The Wisdom of Imperfection*, pp. 220-226.
49 Kurtz, *Body-Centered Psychotherapy: The Hakomi Method*, p. 43.

50 I refer the reader back to the comments in Chapter 2 where I describe Jung's notion of the Self as a metaphorical center of our totality akin to a sense of our buddha nature. There is no intention to define some form of self-existent Atman. In this respect the notion of Self is merely imputed upon an inner notion of a center of totality often felt as a deeper root of meaning and intention.

51 From the prayer of the four immeasurable thoughts, the Brahmavihāras.

52 This is not to say there are not times when such medications as antidepressants are the best course of action.

53 From the prayer of the four immeasurables.

54 Consider Wilber's "pre-trans fallacy."

55 A seed syllable is a Sanskrit sound syllable seen as the root or seed from which the deity emerges. In the case of Chenrezig, it is the syllable *Hrih*.

56 Roach, *The Tibetan Book of Yoga*.

57 From the *Heruka Sadhana* of Pabongka Rinpoche.

58 Jung, *Symbols of Transformation*, p. 225.

59 See Preece, *The Wisdom of Imperfection*, Chapter 4.

60 Arya Maitreya and Asanga, *The Changeless Nature*, p. 31.

61 This is a paraphrase of Murray Cox's expression regarding poetic metaphor used in psychotherapy.

62 Preece, *The Wisdom of Imperfection*, p. 215.

63 Chögyam Trungpa, *Cutting Through Spiritual Materialism*, p.153.

64 From the *Heruka Sadhana* by Pabongka Rinpoche titled "The Excellent Increase of Great Bliss," translated by Rob Preece: "In order to eliminate the sufferings of sentient beings I offer myself immediately to all the Buddhas."

65 Dharmarakshita, *The Wheel of Sharp Weapons*, verses 1-6.

Bibliography

Arya Maitreya and Asanga. *The Changeless Nature, The Mahayana Uttara Tantra Shastra.* Trans. Ken and Katia Holmes. Eskdalemuir, Dumfriesshire, Scotland: Kagyu Samye Ling, 1985.

Batchelor, Stephen. *Buddhism Without Beliefs: A Contemporary Guide to Awakening.* London: Bloomsbury, 1998.

Batchelor, Stephen. *Flight: An Existential Concept of Buddhism.* Delhi: Buddhist Publication Society, 1984.

Campbell, Joseph. *Myths to Live By.* New York: Viking, 1972.

Chodron, Thubten. *Guided Meditations on the Stages of the Path.* Ithaca, N.Y.: Snow Lion Publications, 2007.

Dalai Lama. *A Human Approach to World Peace.* London: Wisdom Publications, 1984.

Dalai Lama. *Stages of Meditation.* Ithaca, N.Y.: Snow Lion Publications, 2001.

Dalai Lama. *Universal Responsibility and the Good Heart.* Dharamsala, India: Library of Tibetan Works and Archives, 1976.

Dhargyey, Geshe Ngawang. *The Tibetan Tradition of Mental Development.* Dharamsala, India: Library of Tibetan Works and Archives, 1974.

Dharmarakshita. *The Wheel of Sharp Weapons: A Mahayana Training of the Mind.* Trans. Geshe Ngawang Dhargyey et al. Dharamsala, India: Library of Tibetan Works and Archives, 1981.

Edinger, Edward F. *Ego and Archetype.* Boston: Shambhala, 1992.

Hillman, James. *Anima: An Anatomy of a Personified Notion.* Dallas: Spring Publications, 1985.

Johnson, Robert A. *He: Understanding Masculine Psychology.* New York: Harper and Row, 1989.

Johnson, Robert A. *She: Understanding Feminine Psychology.* New York: Perennial Library, 1989.

Johnson, Robert A. *We: Understanding the Psychology of Romantic Love.* San Francisco: Harper and Row, 1983.

Jung, C. G. *The Archetypes and the Collective Unconscious.* The Collected Works of C. G. Jung, vol. 9, part 1. Bollingen Series. Princeton, N.J.: Princeton University Press, 1971.

Jung, C. G. *Psychology and Alchemy*. The Collected Works of C. G. Jung, vol. 12. London: Routledge & Kegan Paul, 1980.

Jung, C. G. *Psychology and Religion*. The Collected Works of C. G. Jung, vol. 11. London: Routledge & Kegan Paul, 1969.

Jung, C. G. *Psychology and the East*. Princeton, N.J.: Princeton University Press, 1978.

Jung, C. G. *The Structure and Dynamics of the Psyche*. The Collected Works of C. G. Jung, vol. 8. London: Routledge & Kegan Paul, 1969.

Jung, C. G. *Symbols of Transformation*. The Collected Works of C. G. Jung, vol. 5. Bollingen Series. Princeton, N.J.: Princeton University Press, 1976.

Jung, C. G. *Two Essays on Analytical Psychology*. The Collected Works of C. G. Jung, vol. 7. London: Routledge & Kegan Paul, 1966.

Jung, C. G., ed. *Man and His Symbols*. London: Picador, 1978.

Jung, Emma. *Animus and Anima*. Dallas: Spring Publications, 1985.

Kurtz, Ron. *Body-Centered Psychotherapy: The Hakomi Method*. Mendocino, Calif.: LifeRhythm, 1990.

Levine, Peter A., with Ann Frederick. *Waking the Tiger: Healing Trauma: The Innate Capacity to Transform Overwhelming Experiences*. Berkeley, Calif.: North Atlantic Books, 1997.

Longchenpa. *The Four-Themed Precious Garland: An Introduction to Dzog-Chen, the Great Completeness*. Trans. Alexander Berzin et al. Dharamsala, India: Library of Tibetan Works and Archives, 1979.

Longchenpa. *Kindly Bent to Ease Us*. 3 vols. Trans. Herbert V. Guenther. Berkeley, Calif.: Dharma Publishing, 1975-1976.

Miller, Alice. *The Drama of Being a Child: The Search for the True Self*. London: Virago, 1991.

Miller, Alice. *Thou Shalt Not Be Aware: Society's Betrayal of the Child*. London: Pluto Press, 1984.

Otto, Walter F. *Dionysus: Myth and Cult*. Dallas: Spring Publications, 1965.

Pearson, Carol. S. *The Hero Within: Six Archetypes We Live By*. San Francisco: HarperSanFrancisco, 1986.

Preece, Rob. *The Psychology of Buddhist Tantra*. Ithaca, N.Y.: Snow Lion Publications, 2006. Previously published under the title *The Alchemical Buddha*. Devon, U.K.: Mudra, 2000.

Preece, Rob. *The Wisdom of Imperfection: The Challenge of Individuation in Buddhist Life*. Ithaca, N.Y.: Snow Lion Publications, 2006.

Rabten, Geshe. *The Essential Nectar: Meditations on the Buddhist Path*. Boston: Wisdom Publications, 1984.

Rabten, Geshe. *The Preliminary Practices of Tibetan Buddhism*. Dharamsala, India: Library of Tibetan Works and Archives, 1974.

Rabten, Geshe, and Geshe Dhargyey. *Advice from a Spiritual Friend*. Delhi: Publications for Wisdom Culture, 1977.

Roach, Geshe Michael. *The Tibetan Book of Yoga*. New York: Doubleday, 2003.

Rycroft, Charles. *Anxiety and Neurosis*. Harmondsworth, U.K.: Penguin, 1971.

Shantideva. *A Guide to the Bodhisattva's Way of Life*. Trans. Stephen Batchelor. Dharamsala, India: Library of Tibetan Works and Archives, 1979.

Sonam Rinchen, Geshe. *The Three Principal Aspects of the Path*. Trans. and ed. Ruth Sonam. Ithaca, N.Y.: Snow Lion Publications, 1999.

Stein, Murray. *In Midlife: A Jungian Perspective*. Dallas: Spring Publications, 1983.

Stevens, Anthony. *Archetype: A Natural History of the Self*. London: Routledge & Kegan Paul, 1990.

Stevens, Anthony. *On Jung*. London: Penguin, 1991.

Storr, Anthony. *The Art of Psychotherapy*. Oxford: Butterworth-Heinemann, 1994.

Tarthang Tulku. *Openness Mind*. Emeryville, Calif.: Dharma Publishing, 1978.

Thogme Zangpo. *The Thirty-seven Practices of All Buddhas' Sons*. Trans. Geshe Ngawang Dhargyey et al. Dharamsala, India: Library of Tibetan Works and Archives, 1973.

Trungpa, Chögyam. *Cutting Through Spiritual Materialism*. Boston: Shambhala, 1987.

Tsong-kha-pa. *The Great Treatise on the Stages of the Path to Enlightenment*. 3 vols. Trans. Lamrim Chenmo Translation Committee. Ed. Joshua W. C. Cutler and Guy Newland. Ithaca, N.Y.: Snow Lion Publications, 2000-2004.

Washburn, Michael. *The Ego and the Dynamic Ground*. Albany, N.Y.: State University of New York Press, 1995.

Welwood, John. *Awakening the Heart*. Boston: Shambhala, 1985.

Welwood, John. *Towards a Psychology of Awakening*. Boston: Shambhala, 2002.

Winnicott, D. W. *The Maturational Processes and the Facilitating Environment: Studies in the Theory of Emotional Development*. London: Karnac Books, 1980.

Yeshe, Lama Thubten. *Becoming the Compassion Buddha*. Boston: Wisdom Publications, 2003.

Yeshe, Lama Thubten. *Introduction to Tantra: The Transformation of Desire*. Boston: Wisdom Publications, 1987.

Yeshe, Lama Thubten. *Mahamudra*. Boston: Wisdom Publications, 1981.

Yeshe, Lama Thubten. *The Tantric Path of Purification: The Yoga Method of Heruka Vajrasattva Including Complete Retreat Instructions*. Boston: Wisdom Publications, 1995.

Yeshe, Lama Thubten. *Wisdom Energy 2*. Boston: Wisdom Publications, 1979.

Zopa Rinpoche. *The Wish-fulfilling Golden Sun*. Kathmandu, Nepal: Kopan Monastery, 1973.